1970

DANTE

BOOKS BY HENRY DWIGHT SEDGWICK

ITALY IN THE THIRTEENTH CENTURY

A SHORT HISTORY OF ITALY

AN APOLOGY FOR OLD MAIDS AND OTHER ESSAYS

ESSAYS ON GREAT WRITERS

LIFE OF FRANCIS PARKMAN, ETC.

DANTE

AN ELEMENTARY BOOK FOR THOSE
WHO SEEK IN THE GREAT POET THE
TEACHER OF SPIRITUAL LIFE

BY
HENRY DWIGHT SEDGWICK

NEW HAVEN
YALE UNIVERSITY PRESS
LONDON: HUMPHREY MILFORD
OXFORD UNIVERSITY PRESS
MDCCCCXVIII

TO

S. M. S.

Qual vuol gentil donna parere
Vada con lei.

O Friend, hope in Him while thou livest,
   know Him while thou livest,
   For in life is thy release.
If thy bonds be not broken while thou livest,
   What hope of deliverance in death?

    .   .   .   .

If He is found now, He is found then:
   If not, we go but to dwell in the city of Death.
If thou hast union now, thou shalt have it hereafter.

    .   .   .   .

Kabir saith: It is the spirit of the quest that helpeth.
   I am the slave of the spirit of the quest.

                             (Kabir)

Notre cœur est plus grand que tout le monde.
                    St. François de Sales

Our whole doctrine is nothing else but an instruction to
show how man may create a Kingdom of light within himself.
                        Jacob Boehme

PREFACE

ANOTHER elementary book on Dante needs an excuse. My excuse is that interest in Dante among people who have not the time or the inclination to become serious students is very widespread, more so perhaps than ever before, and that as these people feel various sorts of curiosity about Dante, there may be those among them whose attitude towards Dante coincides with mine.

Some readers are eager to learn about the political turmoil in which he lived, about Guelphs and Ghibellines, about Blacks and Whites, about Pope Boniface VIII and Prince Philip of Valois. Others are drawn to Dante's theology, to mediaeval Christianity, to the doctrines of Albertus Magnus, Bonaventura, and Thomas Aquinas; others still are chiefly concerned with Dante's exposition of mediaeval science, his geography, the Ptolemaic astronomy, and similar matters; and so on, through a wide range of taste and curiosity. All such readers can find on any library shelf any number of books from which to slake their thirst. For centuries scholars have been delving in the past to unearth facts about Dante's life, to discover explanations for the references and allusions in the *Divine Comedy*, and to trace the sources of his learning. The early commentators, Boccaccio, Benvenuto da Imola, Francesco da Buti, and their successors, the moderns, Witte, Ozanam, Scartazzini, our illustrious American scholars, Longfellow, Lowell, Norton, and those of more recent date, Torraca, Casini, Zingarelli, Hauvette, Gardner, Toynbee, Moore, Wicksteed, Oelsner, Fletcher, Grandgent, and others, with pious seriousness have been busy studying not only the world, but the whole universe, in which Dante lived, so that we may be able in imagination to put ourselves by his side, see what he saw, and comprehend the hopes, beliefs, and passions of his time.

Nevertheless, there must be in every generation persons whose experiences in life are different from those of scholars, whose demands upon life are different from the demands made upon life by scholars, and who therefore seek in a great poet an aspect other than that which commonly reveals itself to the learned. Of such seekers some at least desire to forsake the highroad of erudition, to shake themselves free from authorized guides, and to obtain for themselves a more personal intimacy with Dante's spirit, and therefore there is always a chance that what a man, not a scholar, gets from Dante may contain a hint to help others, who likewise are not scholars, adjust their relations with the great poet more to their satisfaction than they would be able to do under learned guidance. The hand of little employment, in some respects, has the daintier sense; and there may be a value in the impressions made upon the uninstructed, fresher mind of the passer-by, who, free from all ambition of adding to the high scaffolding of knowledge that has been built up so admirably about Dante, has sought, not pleasure, but help and comfort from merely touching, as it were, the garment of a great man.

In these years we are living through a period that seems the handiwork of the Spirit of Evil, as if the Almighty had said to Satan, "Put forth thine hand, behold all that man hath is within thy power," and we turn to the great spiritual leaders of the world as never before. For many the traditional doctrines of Christianity have lost much, or all, of their power; the comfort that depends upon supernatural virtue has lost its soothing; and the precepts of Stoicism are not enough to give us courage to look upon the world as we see it. We must have some ideal world in our mind's eye, on the creation of which we may labor and sacrifice ourselves. In order to do this we must get spiritual power where we can; and Dante stands ready to help us. Not only now, but in the years after the war we shall all need spiritual support, for history seems to teach that after great wars people turn their minds to material things, to eating, drinking, and being merry, to the acceptance of luxury, ease, and comfort as the goal of man, and shut their eyes to things of the spirit.

For these reasons, it seems to me likely that, at the present time, here and there, persons who lack interest in the Middle Ages, who remain cold before the assertion that Dante is "the voice of ten silent centuries," or "the synthesis of mediaeval thought," may find some use for a primer which leaves learning one side and busies itself with Dante as a poet and a believer in eternal righteousness.

H. D. S.

TABLE OF CONTENTS

xiii

CHAPTER I

DANTE'S FAME

TO us of the Western World, certainly to English-speaking people, bred upon the traditions of Protestant Christianity, the Bible is the book first in rank, supreme over all other books. It is the base and prop of the Christian religion, it has played a guiding part in the world's history, and, in the English version, it is the great prose classic of all literature. No poetry nor prose can contest its primacy. What book can venture to claim the second place, unless it be the *Divine Comedy?*

The Bishop of Ripon, Boyd Carpenter, says, diffidently as becomes a man who speaks with authority, that although Dante is not the greatest poet, yet the *Divine Comedy* is the greatest poem we possess. He might well have made the assertion more boldly; for what single book is there, leaving the Bible aside, in the whole range of literature that, in height, depth, and amplitude of thought, in ethical, philosophical, and religious interest, in intensity and variety of human drama, can match the *Divine Comedy?* Take the *Iliad* or the *Odyssey;* great and beautiful as they are, nevertheless we, who are bred upon near two thousand years of Christian beliefs, find in them little ethical and less religious meaning. We ask of a great book that it shall take us up on a tower, as it were, show us wider regions of life than of ourselves we can perceive, and, by the illumination of that wider knowledge, help us to choose our own path with a truer sense of what is good in life.

Take any play of Aeschylus, Euripides, or Sophocles, and not only is the thought in great measure alien, but the powerful concentration of interest on one situation or one passion is so solemn, so remote, so unalloyed by common, human triviality, that it does not satisfy the various demands which we, of less robust souls than the ancient Hellenes, make upon literature as the interpreter of life. Take the *Aeneid* or *De Rerum Natura*, and it needs no second thought to see that neither Virgil nor Lucretius can feed the hungry soul. Take *King Lear*, *Othello*, or *Macbeth;* the play ousts us from ourselves, it exalts us into a world of passion high above our own world, and causes us rather to forget ourselves than to ennoble our own spiritual needs. *Hamlet* is but an exposition of the helplessness of man in striving to bring his life into right relations with the eternal. Goethe's *Faust* has both human passion and philosophy; it has poetry and the grand manner; but in variety, in religious reach, in helping us to put our little hands into a great helper's hand, it cannot claim — perhaps it would disdain — comparison with the *Commedia*. Even in *Faust* Goethe does not divest himself of his theory that self-dependence should be the goal of a man's effort. In French literature there is no book that professes so wide a scope of human interest as Dante's poem, and none that can compare with its poetry. So, too, *Don Quixote*, however profound, however filled with the nobility as well as with the irony of life, is not a poem.

In each one of these masterpieces of literature there may well be some point or points in which they match, or even excel, the *Divine Comedy*, but in the combination of grandeur, vividness, tenderness, and beauty, at least for a person who seeks to find a meaning in life and to set himself in right relations with the universe, the *Divine Comedy* is easily superior, and has clear title to a rank inferior only to the Bible.

The poem usually put forward in comparison with the *Divine Comedy* is *Paradise Lost*. This is no place to push comparisons and weigh spiritual and poetic merits; and yet two things may be suggested. Lord Macaulay states somewhere, that Milton's reputation would stand higher had *Paradise Lost* ended with the fourth book. One need not accept Macaulay as an authority upon poetry, one need not agree with his statement, but his position may certainly be supported by argument; whereas, with the *Divine Comedy*, the whole structure of the poem, canto upon canto, culminating at the end of the *Paradiso* in the sublime fulfillment of the soul's desire, is so excellently contrived that nobody could suggest that any taking from it would be other than a mutilation. The second suggestion is that Milton's theology is now of no living interest, whereas the fundamental religious doctrine in the *Divine Comedy* is fraught with as much meaning for us to-day as for Dante's contemporaries six hundred years ago.

The career of the *Divine Comedy* has been worthy
of its rank. Even in Dante's lifetime, great noblemen
were interested in the poem, and unlettered people
declaimed bits of it in the streets. Within a few
years after his death commentators began to explain the meaning of the poem, in Florence, in
Bologna, and elsewhere. The poet's two sons, Pietro and Jacopo, both wrote glosses; Pietro, who followed the profession of law in Verona, composed
his in very elaborate fashion. Giovanni Villani, the
historian, a contemporary, inserted in his history
of Florence a little sketch of the poet. To receive a
place beside kings in a national chronicle at that
time was an unprecedented honor for a man of
letters. Not long afterwards Boccaccio (1313–1375)
wrote his biography of Dante. Boccaccio is known to
most of us as the author of the *Decameron*, and is
burdened with the reputation of having written
stories best left unwritten. This is a sorry piece of
injustice. No doubt Boccaccio in his youth followed
primrose paths; but his contemporaries knew him
as a poet, as a distinguished scholar, and as a man
chosen by his government to perform responsible
services for the state. He was a devoted friend to
Petrarch and a reverent admirer of Dante. He is
accused of regarding biography as a branch of the
art of fiction; and it is true that he sometimes let his
pen run away with him, and that he had little or no
idea of investigation or critical examination in writing biography. But he was a Florentine, already
eight years old when Dante died, was acquainted
with Dante's daughter and with persons who had

known Dante, and his biography, though it wanders away from its subject somewhat whimsically, is the best early biography of Dante that there is. Later, at the instance of the government of Florence, Boccaccio delivered public lectures upon the *Comedy*, but owing to ill health he got no further than the seventeenth canto of the *Inferno*. A year or two afterwards, Benvenuto da Imola, who had attended Boccaccio's lectures, lectured upon the *Comedy* in Bologna. These lectures were subsequently cast into the form of a commentary, in Latin. This commentary is very long, and full of discursive, historical information; it has been published in half a dozen great folio volumes by William Warren Vernon, and constitutes one of the great monuments in the literature upon Dante. A few years later Filippo Villani, a nephew of Giovanni Villani, wrote a little book of lives of famous citizens of Florence, which included a brief biography of Dante.

In the fifteenth century, during the rise of the Renaissance in Florence, three biographies were written, by Leonardo Bruni (1369–1444), Giannozzo Manetti (1396–1459), and Giovan Mario Filelfo (1426–1480). Of these Leonardo Bruni's is the most valuable. Besides this interest shown in Dante's life, Cristoforo Landino (1424–1504), one of the early Florentine Platonists, a scholar and statesman, and also both tutor and friend to Lorenzo dei Medici, wrote another commentary on the *Commedia*. The great painter, Sandro Botticelli (1447–1515), made illustrations of the three canticles, *Hell*, *Purgatory*, and *Paradise*. And Michelangelo, who of all Italians

comes nearest to Dante in intellectual power and
magnanimity of soul, wrote this sonnet upon the
poet, for whom he entertained a passionate reverence:

> Dal mondo scese ai ciechi abissi, e poi
>   Che l'uno e l'altro inferno vide, a Dio,
>   Scorto dal gran pensier, vivo salìo;
>   E ne diè in terra vero lume a noi.
> Stella d'alto valor, co' raggi suoi
>   Gli occulti eterni a noi ciechi scoprìo;
>   E n'ebbe il premio alfin, che il mondo rio
>   Dona sovente ai più pregiati eroi.
> Di Dante mal fur l'opre conosciute,
>   E'l bel desìo, da quel popolo ingrato,
>   Che solo ai giusti manca di salute.
> Pur foss'io tal! chè, a simil sorte nato,
>   Per l'aspro esilio suo con la virtute
>   Darei del mondo il più felice stato.

> From out the world he went down to the blind abyss,
>   And, after he had seen all Hell throughout,
>   Escorted by great thought, mounted alive
>   To God, and gave true gleams of Him to us on earth.
> This star of virtue, by his shining showed
>   To us blind men the hid eternities;
>   And that reward received, which this bad world
>   On its most valiant heroes frequently bestows.
> The poem of Dante and his noble hope
>   Were but ill known to that ungrateful folk
>   Who only good men fail to recognize.
> Could I be such as he, born to like deeds,
>   I'd give the happiest state in all the world
>   For his harsh exile with such virtue joined.

During the seventeenth and eighteenth centuries
the intellectual world of Italy, turning toward the
classic, and then to the baroque and the rococo,

looked down on the Middle Ages as barbaric, and consequently neglected Dante; but as the great human movement that expressed itself most dramatically in the French Revolution began to affect Italy, interest in Dante revived and quickened; and since the beginning of the Risorgimento Dante has been a kind of guardian genius watching over Italy, as reverence-inspiring a figure to Italians as Pallas Athene was to the imagination of the men of Athens. His influence in Italy has been twofold. In the first place (followed in the next generation by Petrarch and Boccaccio, who carried on the literary task that he began), he directed the course and shaped the form of Italian literature. He found Italy divided up into numberless independent regions, each speaking its own dialect, and here and there local schools of poetry, but no national literature. By his poetry and his prose he raised the dialect of Florence to be the language of Italy. He is the creator of the Italian literary language to a degree that no other man in any country, not even Luther in Germany, can boast of. And in addition to that, it may be said of him, without exaggeration, that he is the founder of United Italy. He gave to the people of the Italian peninsula, who were divided and separate, subject to all sorts of petty governments of King, Pope, Duke, Seigniory, Doge, Baron, the promise of political unity by giving Italy, as it were, a soul. He has been her spiritual banner. From him were learned the passionate convictions that Italy should be free and united. He has been the rallying center of all Italian patriotism. Alfieri, who calls him "O gran padre Alighier," Leopardi, Ugo Foscolo, Carducci, and all the high aspiring souls of the Risorgimento, turned towards him. And besides all this, Dante has held and holds an unrivaled place in the religious life of Italy. The policy of the Roman Catholic Church has been to discourage private reading of the Bible, and the *Divine Comedy* has stepped in and occupies the place with them that the Bible holds with us. It is the book for them that concerns the dealings of God with man.

From Italy Dante's fame spread rapidly over Europe. In the beginning of the fifteenth century Spain felt his influence, and translations appeared in Castilian and Catalan. In France, because her enthusiasm for Italy was first kindled by the Italian Renaissance, interest in Dante lingered, and the French did not begin to appreciate him until the period of Catholic reawakening in the nineteenth century, when the two religious writers and scholars, Lamennais and Ozanam, proclaimed his genius. In Germany Karl Witte (1800–1883) stands at the head of all Dante scholars. His *Dante-Forschungen* constitutes the greatest contribution to our knowledge concerning Dante and the *Divine Comedy* that has been made since the fourteenth century; and since then there have been many distinguished German Dantists. Among the living Karl Vossler is eminent. Karl Witte and the scholarly King of Saxony, John Nepomuk Maria Joseph, who wrote under the pseudonym of Philalethes, both published translations of the *Comedy*. Scartazzini, the German Swiss, is probably the best known of recent foreign commentators, though Mr. Norton said that he lacked "the higher qualities" of the critic.

Dante's fame seems to have reached England earlier than any other country. Chaucer knew the *Divine Comedy* well. Some of the Elizabethans were more or less acquainted with it; Sir Philip Sidney for one, and probably Edmund Spenser. Since then almost all the greater English poets, certainly all who were scholars (as so many English poets have been), have admired and cherished Dante, — Milton, Gray, Shelley, Byron, Wordsworth, Tennyson, Browning. The earliest translation that still holds the field, by the Rev. Henry Francis Cary, was begun about 1797, and published early in the nineteenth century. In the next generation Thomas Carlyle wrote his celebrated essay on Dante and Shakespeare (the "Hero as a Poet"); and his brother John made a prose translation of the *Inferno* that has become a classic. Dante Gabriel Rossetti rendered the *Vita Nuova* into English prose and English verse as nearly equal in beauty to the original as the difference of language would permit. And a long line of English scholars, Lord Vernon, his son W. W. Vernon, Dean Church, Dean Plumptre, Edward Moore, A. J. Butler, E. G. Gardner, Paget Toynbee, P. H. Wicksteed, Oelsner, and others have devoted their talents and industry to a study of the great poet.

In the United States perhaps T. W. Parsons is entitled to the credit of leadership. He was followed by the three eminent scholars whose names are associated with Harvard University. Longfellow not only translated the *Divine Comedy* but also wrote long notes of explanation. Lowell's essay on Dante is famous; and Charles Eliot Norton translated the *Comedy* and the *Vita Nuova* and dedicated a great part of his Italian scholarship to the service of Dante. Since then there have been several translations by Americans; that by the late Henry Johnson of Yale University met with hearty approval from many Dante lovers, and a new translation by Professor Courtney Langdon of Brown University, of which the *Inferno* only has appeared, is excellent. Besides translations, frequent books of criticism, of investigation, of explanation, as well as essays and lectures, testify to the living power of the great poet.

Aside from the special grounds for his exalted position in Italy, the reasons for the universal interest in Dante are that he is a great poet and a great prophet of righteousness. As a poet, he is one of the supreme masters of language. He takes the soft, voweled, Italian syllables and gives them a temper and rugged force equal to the German of Luther's Bible or the English of *Pilgrim's Progress*. And, though we usually think of Italian as words of many syllables, with Dante one word in every three is a monosyllable. This mingling words of different lengths, measured by syllables, gives flexibility and power to his verse. And though the Italian language labors under what to English ears is the disadvantage that almost all its words end in vowels, yet Dante, by freely clipping off the final vowels, out of sweetness brings forth strength, and creates a sense of power that has never been surpassed, if it has been equaled, in English. His ear is musical and he loves the melody of his native, liquid syllables; and yet he uses their music unconsciously, or by an art so mastered in his youth as to have become instinctive. He concentrates his mind upon his thought, and often disregards his mode of expression, or, with a violence that Italians call *terribilità*, forces his words to fit his thought. In his tender passages he gives free rein to his genius for beauty, but he does not calculate the succession of consonants, or the repetition, or contrast of vowels, as lesser poets do. His harmonies, even his rare alliterations, spring from his love of music.

Dante also possesses the magic secret of arranging words — familiar words in daily use — in such an order that they conjure up images of all kinds, of horror or loathsomeness, of beauty and tenderness, so vividly that the reader feels were he to put out his hand he would touch them. There is no need to dwell upon this; the charm he has exercised upon English poets — on Chaucer, Milton, Byron, Shelley, Coleridge, Browning — is proof enough. Byron said: "There is no tenderness equal to the tenderness of Dante"; Coleridge: "In picturesqueness Dante is beyond all other poets, ancient or modern"; and Shelley speaks of "the exquisite tenderness, sensibility, and ideal beauty in which Dante excelled all poets except Shakspere." [1]

Dante is very great as a poet, but as a poet he has rivals, whereas as a prophet of righteousness he has no peer since the time of the Apostles. It is for this reason that the book of Isaiah and St. Paul's Epistles

[1] *Dante in English Literature*, Toynbee.

are an almost necessary preparation for understanding the *Divine Comedy*. He is the best medicine
for minds diseased with skepticism as to the value
of righteousness.

Sometime or other in the ears of almost all people
who meet the ordinary experiences of life, the voice
of Mephistopheles, the Spirit-that-denies, sounds
most persuasively. He smiles his pleasant, mocking
smile at all the convictions we learned when we were
children, as though they were merely the convictions
of children; he smiles at all we have been taught in
school, at church, at home, about honor, loyalty,
holiness, and, with a great show of reason, asks why
it is that a man should grunt and sweat for his
fellow-men; why should he give up the delights of
life for the sake of ideas foisted upon us by ages of
superstition; why should he go and stand in a trench
in Flanders on behalf of the Belgians; why should
he give his health, his youth, his life, for his country?
What is "country" but a motley collection of two-
legged animals who happen to live under one political
government?

In upon this state of mind Dante sweeps like an
archangel and speaks, as when God spoke out of the
whirlwind. He is filled with the Spirit-that-affirms.
"Pleasure, ease, enjoyment! (he would cry) How
dare a man mention such words, when to him has
been given the priceless privilege of life, an opportunity to fight for righteousness, to serve God,
to feel the joy of an uplifted soul?" Dante cannot
comprehend and cannot endure a pusillanimous,
effeminate state of mind. And, therefore, many

people, in moments of doubt or disbelief, especially in these dark days, find strength and comfort from his masculine energy and his heroic soul. His fame rests secure in the permanent needs of the human soul for poetry, heroism, and holiness.

CHAPTER II

THE PROPHET AND HIS WORLD

DANTE ALIGHIERI was born in Florence in the year 1265. He belonged to that doubtful generation that may be regarded as the last generation of the Middle Ages or the first of the Modern World. It was a time of turmoil; the old order had rotted away, and the new order, pushing up through the broken crust of the past, was still too rudimentary and unsubstantial to be recognized by contemporary eyes. The world of politics was topsy-turvy. Stable government there was none. In this clash of old and new, Dante clung to the past. He turned his face backwards, and believed that he saw through the arch of centuries, in radiant light, a universal government of law, order, and justice, — an imperial rule, which by the mere majesty of its presence enabled mankind to attain complete development, intellectual, moral, and spiritual. For him Rome was what Israel was for the Hebrew prophets. According to his creed, the Roman Empire had been established by the Lord to carry out His divine purpose for the government of the world; Aeneas, like Moses, had led the children of a covenant into a promised land. Sign upon sign, miracle upon miracle had shown that the Romans, "holy, compassionate and glorious," were God's chosen people (*De Mon.* Book II). The heroes of the Republic, the founder of the Empire, Julius Caesar, and his successors, the "good" Augustus (*Inf.* I, 71), Trajan, "prince of high glory" (*Purg.* X, 73), Justinian (*Par.* VI), Charlemagne, emperor after emperor, whether Latin, Greek, or Teuton, down to the illustrious House of Hohenstaufen (*V. E.* I, ch. 12), were all servants of God, and, in establishing and maintaining the Roman Empire, had performed His will. In Dante's judgment, it was patent to everybody, by clear-cut "demonstration, that the Emperor, or Monarch of the world, is in direct relation to the Prince of the Universe, who is God" (*De Mon.* III, ch. 16). In no way other than by submission to this universal Empire could mankind realize the best that it is capable of; by general obedience to this universal Empire only could peace, justice, law, and order be set up throughout the world. But right does not make might. The ancient sovereignty, that looked so solid and splendid to Dante as he cast his eyes backward, had cracked and shrunk. Interregnums, rival claims, negligent princes had put the little that was left of imperial authority in jeopardy, and had brought ruin upon Italy, the fairest of imperial provinces. No man then alive, looking at the foul disorder in which she lay, could guess that Italy had been, and of right still was, the great foundation, the origin and crown, of the Roman Empire. As men to-day who have visited Belgium are shaken in their most familiar notions of the stability of right, so Dante was shaken and

sick at heart at the confusion of Italy; and the
bitterness in his soul increased because in a universe
where justice and mercy are signs of righteousness,
confusion is the sign of sin. In like manner Isaiah had
felt for Israel:

Ah sinful nation, a people laden with iniquity,
A seed of evil-doers, children that deal corruptly:
They have forsaken the Lord,
They have despised the Holy One of Israel;
They are estranged and gone backward. . . .
Your country is desolate; your cities are burned with fire,
Your land, strangers devour it in your presence,
And it is desolate, as overthrown by strangers.

Isaiah i, 4–7

With the death of the Emperor Frederick II (1250)
the Roman Empire had collapsed. The last imperial
family, the Hohenstaufens, had been cut off by their
enemies, root and branch, and the German princes
who succeeded Frederick II concerned themselves
wholly with Germany and their own personal for-
tunes, leaving Italy a prey to anarchy. Everywhere throughout the peninsula there was jealousy,
hatred, and war. In Lombardy, each city — Milan,
Pavia, Parma, Cremona — fought with its neighbor; in Tuscany, Florence, Siena, Arezzo, Lucca,
Pistoia did the same; Rome fought the little
cities roundabout; the kingdom of Naples was split
in two, and Sicily fought the mainland; outside
the walled towns, feudal barons sallied forth from
castles, perched on outlying hills of the Alps or
Apennines, and robbed and laid waste in savage
fury; and on the waters that encompass Italy the

armed galleys of Venice, Genoa, and Pisa sunk one
another. And as city fought against city, so within
each town political party fought against political
party, class against class, family against family. In
an apostrophe to Italy Dante says:

> Ahi serva Italia, di dolore ostello,
> > nave senza nocchiero in gran tempesta,
> > non donna di provincie, ma bordello!
> . . . .
>
> ed ora in te non stanno senza guerra
> > li vivi tuoi, e l'un l'altro si rode
> > di quei che un muro ed una fossa serra.
> Cerca, misera, intorno dalle prode
> > le tue marine, e poi ti guarda in seno,
> > se alcuna parte in te di pace gode.
>
> Ah, Italy! Thou slave, thou ostelry of woe!
> > Ship without pilot in a mighty storm,
> > She that was once a princess among provinces
> How now become a brothel!
> . . . .
>
> They that now dwell in thee are all at war:
> > Even men encompassed by one wall, one moat,
> > Rend each the other. Search, wretched Italy,
> Along thy seashore, over every coast,
> > And in thy bosom look, to find
> > If any place in thee enjoyeth peace.
> > > > > > *Purg.* VI, 76–87

The weight of lawlessness lay heavy on the land;
but the fault, according to Dante, was not due to the
political institution of empire contrived by Providence, but to the derelictions of negligent Emperors.
And the Emperors were not alone in blame. Another
mighty edifice had been created and built up by

Providence for the welfare of mankind, the Holy
Roman Apostolic Church. Christ had given to Peter,
and his successors, power over spiritual things,
symbolized by the keys of heaven; He had established His Church to be the ark of His covenant for
all the world; but the guardians to whom the ark
had been committed were not faithful to their trust.
Instead of keeping their hearts and minds fixed on
the things of heaven, they had succumbed to the
itchings of covetousness. Pope Sylvester had accepted from the Emperor Constantine a great grant
of temporal power and possessions (*Inf.* XIX, 115–
117). That fatal grant was the beginning of worldliness; and worldliness had grown by what it fed
upon. Christ had said: "Provide neither gold, nor
silver, nor brass in your purses, nor scrip for your
journey" (*De Mon.* III, X, 109–110); and yet, in
flat disobedience to His command, priests, prelates,
popes, had turned their backs on the concerns of
the soul and sought for earthly riches and earthly
dominion. Peter and Paul had gone about lean and
unshod, taking food when and where it might be
given to them, but priests of mediaeval Italy went
heavily laden with possessions (*Par.* XXI, 127–132);
the popes Nicholas III (1277–1280) and Boniface
VIII (1294–1303) set terrible examples of selling the
gifts of the spirit for money (*Inf.* XIX). They had
polluted the papacy, as had been foretold by St.
John the Divine in the Apocalypse: "I saw a woman
sit upon a scarlet-coloured beast, full of names of
blasphemy . . . and the woman was arrayed in
purple and scarlet-colour, and decked with gold and

precious stones and pearls, having a golden cup in her hand full of abominations and filthiness" (Rev. xvii, 3–4, *Inf.* XIX, 106–109).

Love of comfort, ease, luxury, power, had infected the Church. And worse than this, the Papacy had not only not performed its own duty, but it had thwarted the Empire in doing its duty. Providence had assigned to each its task. The Emperor's duty was to enforce law and order, — he was the supreme temporal lord of the world; the Pope's duty was to instruct and guide men's souls, — he was the supreme spiritual lord. Their functions were separate and distinct; but the Popes had not only opposed the Emperors in temporal matters and encouraged and stirred up rebellion against them, but even assumed imperial functions themselves, converting their sacred office into a secular government. They had debased religion and confounded temporal matters (*Purg.* XVI).

With the Roman Pope thwarting and fighting the Roman Emperor, how could the people of Florence, who should have been able to live in tranquillity beside their vines and fig trees under the sword of the Emperor and the crook of the Pope, hope to have leisure and opportunity to achieve a higher morality and to pursue a spiritual life? All the good old ways were gone. The old Florence, that had lived in peace, sobriety, and modesty, was a thing of the past. In earlier generations the principal men of the city used to lead lives of frugal dignity; they were too proud to indulge in vulgar luxury; they wore jerkins made of leather, and their wives spun their own linen.

The women lived simply; they tended the cradle
themselves, and told their children stories of how
their ancestors founded Rome and Florence, Rome's
most beautiful daughter; then homes were really
homes (*Par.* XV). But now, in Dante's time, the
women decked themselves with coronets and chains,
they painted their faces, they dressed immodestly.
So had it been in Isaiah's time: "Because the
daughters of Zion are haughty, and walk with
stretched forth necks and wanton eyes, walking and
mincing as they go, and making a tinkling with their
feet: therefore the Lord will smite with a scab the
crown of the head of the daughters of Zion . . . the
Lord will take away the bravery of their anklets, and
the cauls, and the crescents; . . . and the fine linen,
. . . and the veils" (Isaiah, iii, 16–23).

Lowered standards of personal dignity were among
the least of the evils. In the absence of orderly government, in the absence of religion, in the sudden ac-
quisition of riches (*Inf.* XVI, 73), wickedness and
vice flourished malignantly. Men familiarly known in
Florence and in neighboring towns, Pistoia, Lucca,
Siena, Arezzo, were guilty of gluttony and drunken-
ness, of mad anger, of highway robbery, of usury, of
malfeasance in office, of bestial sins; but very few
anywhere in all Italy strove after virtue.

Such was the world as it appeared to Dante when
he looked about him with the disillusioned eyes of
manhood; and, like the prophets of old, his soul cried
out: "Why dost Thou show me iniquity and cause
me to behold grievance?" Like them, he felt the burden of sin; like them, his whole being compelled him,

in the midst of darkness, to search for light; like them, he was filled with an imperious need of believing in a God of order, reason, justice, and mercy, of seeking for Him, of finding and then proclaiming Him. Such is a prophet's nature; such is a prophet's task.

Turning from a troubled world toward the heaven of spiritual peace, is a phenomenon common enough in great souls. It marks a large number of the saints; and both the beginning and the continuance of the process are of absorbing interest. In the case of some men, there is what in popular speech is called conversion, which takes place, on the surface at least, very rapidly, sometimes almost in the twinkling of an eye, and is so obscure in its working that it seems to be the doing of supernatural power. In the case of others, there is a slow series of contributory causes, in which sometimes the heart, sometimes the intellect, is the dominant factor. In almost all the cases we have little or no information beyond what the persons converted tell us themselves. Of Isaiah's illumination we know nothing except that, as he says, a seraph came and touched his lips with a coal of fire. Of St. Paul we know how his violent nature led him to consent to Stephen's death, how he haled Christians to prison, and how there shined round him a great light from heaven, and he heard a voice say: "Saul, Saul, why persecutest thou me?" St. Augustine tells us of an unpoised and disordered youth, and how, by the way of philosophy, of Plato, Cicero, and St. Paul, he came to where, yearning for truth under the fig tree, he heard a voice saying:

"Tolle lege, tolle lege" — "Take up thy Bible and read." And John Bunyan says "that had not a miracle of grace prevented, I had not only perished by the stroke of eternal justice, but had also laid myself open, even to the stroke of those laws, which bring some to disgrace and open shame before the face of the world" (*Grace Abounding to the Chief of Sinners*), and yet he gives us no exposition of the miracle.

In the lives of these four, Isaiah, St. Paul, St. Augustine, and Bunyan, there was a spiritual crisis that turned them from the carnal life to the spiritual life; but, except in the case of St. Augustine, we know little of the stages that preceded the crisis. With Dante it is different; with him the process of illumination began in his youth and continued all his life. Two great teachers guided his soul and taught him the profoundest lessons of life; one taught him in his youth, the other taught him in his mature years. The first teacher was Beatrice; the second, Exile. Without Beatrice, his eyes would not have been lifted up so high; without Exile, he would not have discovered the inner life in its fullness. So the development of Dante's spiritual life was gradual. In place of a crisis, he underwent growth; and, in the end, arrived face to face with the profoundest realities imaginable by man. The first stage of the long road that he traveled, he has described at length in the *Vita Nuova*. The second stage we know by deductions from the *Commedia* and from casual remarks and references elsewhere. His confessions are nearly as full as those of St. Augustine, and tell in fairly definite sequence and detail the several stages of his spiritual drama.

CHAPTER III

BEATRICE

DANTE'S family — father, mother, brother, and sisters — played little part so far as we know in his life; he mentions a sister (at least such is the interpretation put on one passage of the *Vita Nuova*) but none of the others. We know nothing of any schoolmaster or preceptor except Messer Brunetto Latini, and of him as such only through a passage in the *Inferno*. There Dante says:

in la mente m'è fitta, ed or mi accora,
la cara e buona imagine paterna
di voi, quando nel mondo ad ora ad ora
m'insegnavate come l'uom s'eterna;

Within my memory is fixed, and now it wrings my heart,
Your dear and kindly image, like a father's,
As when in life, from hour to hour, you taught
Me how a man shall have eternal life.

Inf. XV, 82–85

But Brunetto Latini was a distinguished citizen, widely known from his learned books, old enough to be Dante's grandfather, and busy with public affairs, so that the relations between Dante and him could hardly have been more than those between a young man who bore the stamp of genius on his face and the elderly man who recognized the stamp.

What Dante means by the words *"come l'uom
s'eterna"* seems to be a reference to Christ's teaching.
"Behold, one came, and said to him, Good Master,
what good thing shall I do, that I may have eternal
life? And he said unto him, . . . If thou wilt enter
into life, keep the commandments. He saith unto
him, Which? Jesus said, Thou shalt do no murder,
Thou shalt not commit adultery, Thou shalt not
steal, Thou shalt not bear false witness, Honour thy
father and thy mother, and Thou shalt love thy
neighbour as thyself. The young man said unto him,
All these things have I kept from my youth up:
what lack I yet? Jesus said unto him, If thou wilt be
perfect, go and sell that thou hast, and give to the
poor, and thou shalt have treasure in heaven; and
come and follow me" (St. Matt. xix, 16–21). There
could not have been a more tender or beautiful
reference to Brunetto Latini's influence.

The education, however, that molded all his life
came from another source. To him was vouchsafed
in early youth a revelation of the divine, in the form
of a radiant girl. To some men revelation of the divine
has come through sacred books, to others through
some saintly person, to others from the solitude of
the desert, from illness, from a child. There are many
ways from God to the heart of man. Mark Rutherford says: "The love of woman to man is a revelation of the relationship in which God stands to
him. . . . I was wretched till I considered that in her
I saw the Divine Nature itself, and that her passion
was a stream straight from the highest. The love of
woman is, in other words, a living witness never

failing of an actuality in God which otherwise we
should never know" (*Mark Rutherford's Deliverance*,
Ch. VIII). So was it with Dante; only the revelation
lay in his love for Beatrice, rather than in her love
for him. It was Beatrice, not Brunetto Latini, who
started Dante's steps upon the way that leads to the
life of the soul. That she was a real person, seems to
me, though eminent scholars have thought otherwise, beyond a doubt. Dante's own son, Pietro, says
that she was; and Boccaccio, who, though of the
next generation, knew near members of Dante's
family, in his biography tells how they first met, or,
— if we think that he is drawing on his imagination — how they might have met.

Dante's love was not ordinary mortal love. His
love was the love of a poet and saint; for him love
must be a revelation of the grace of God, and he
turned, with all the confidence of innocence, not to
Holy Writ nor to ecclesiastical worship, but to the
girlish loveliness of Beatrice Portinari. As the needs
of his spirit grew deeper, and the power of his spirit
grew stronger, her figure became idealized, crowned
with light, transfigured, until at last, when her
earthly body came to its earthly end, she was translated into the "light between the truth and the intellect," the wisdom of holiness that leads the soul
to God.

In his book, *The New Life*, Dante relates all that
we know of his acquaintance with her: "Nine times
already since my birth had the heaven of light returned to the selfsame point, . . . when first the
glorious Lady of my mind was made manifest to

mine eyes; even she who was called Beatrice by
many who knew not wherefore. . . . She appeared
to me at the beginning of her ninth year almost, and
I saw her almost at the end of my ninth year. Her
dress, on that day was of a most noble colour, a
subdued and goodly crimson, girdled and adorned in
such sort as best suited with her very tender age. At
that moment, I say most truly that the spirit of life,
which hath its dwelling in the secretest chamber of
the heart, began to tremble so violently that the
least pulses of my body shook therewith; and in
trembling it said these words: *Ecce deus fortior me,
qui veniens dominabitur mihi* [Here is a deity stronger
than I, who, coming, shall rule over me], . . . I say
that, from that time forward, Love quite governed
my soul; which was immediately espoused to him,
and with so safe and undisputed a lordship (by virtue
of strong imagination), that I had nothing left for it
but to do all his bidding continually. He oftentimes
commanded me to seek if I might see this youngest
of the Angels: wherefore I in my boyhood often went
in search of her, and found her so noble and praiseworthy that certainly of her might have been said
those words of the poet Homer: 'She seemed not to
be the daughter of a mortal man, but of God.' And
albeit her image, that was with me always, was an
exultation of Love to subdue me, it was yet of so
perfect a quality that it never allowed me to be over-
ruled by Love without the faithful counsel of
reason. . . .

"After the lapse of so many days that nine years
exactly were completed since the above-written

appearance of this most gracious being, on the last
of those days it happened that the same wonderful
lady appeared to me dressed all in pure white, between two gentle ladies elder than she. And passing
through a street, she turned her eyes thither where
I stood sorely abashed: and by her unspeakable
courtesy, which is now guerdoned in the Great
Cycle, she saluted me with so virtuous a bearing that
I seemed then and there to behold the very limits of
blessedness. The hour of her most sweet salutation
was certainly the ninth of that day; and because it
was the first time that any words from her reached
mine ears, I came into such sweetness that I parted
thence as one intoxicated. And betaking me to the
loneliness of mine own room, I fell to thinking of
this most courteous lady, thinking of whom I was
overtaken by a pleasant slumber, wherein a marvel-
ous vision was presented to me." Here he tells of a
vision. Love, of terrible aspect, appeared holding
Beatrice in his arms and Dante's heart in his hand,
and gave Beatrice to eat of the heart and she ate as
one fearing. "From that night forth, the natural
functions of my body began to be vexed and impeded,
for I was given up wholly to thinking of this most
gracious creature: whereby in short space I became
so weak and so reduced that it was irksome to many
of my friends to look upon me; while others, being
moved by spite, went about to discover what it was
my wish should be concealed. Wherefore I (perceiv-
ing the drift of their unkindly questions), by Love's
will, who directed me according to the counsels of
reason, told them how it was Love himself who had

thus dealt with me: and I said so, because the thing was so plainly to be discerned in my countenance that there was no longer any means of concealing it. But when they went on to ask, 'And by whose help hath Love done this?' I looked in their faces smiling, and spake no word in return."

It so happened, that in church one day Dante was gazing at Beatrice, and that another lady, of a pleasant face, sat in a line between him and her, and people, seeing the direction but mistaking the object of his sight, thought that this other lady was his love; and he, learning this, encouraged the error, and, resolving to make use of her as a "screen to the truth," wrote rimes in her honor. But this lady went away to another city, and then at Love's instigation Dante took another "screen" lady to be his protection, "in such sort that the matter was spoken of by many in terms scarcely courteous; through the which I had oftenwhiles many troublesome hours. And by this it happened (to wit: by this false and evil rumour which seemed to misfame me of vice) that she who was the destroyer of all evil and the queen of all good, coming where I was, denied me her most sweet salutation, in the which alone was my blessedness.

"And here it is fitting for me to depart a little from this present matter, that it may be rightly understood of what surpassing virtue her salutation was to me. To the which end I say that when she appeared in any place, it seemed to me, by the hope of her excellent salutation, that there was no man mine enemy any longer; and such warmth of charity came upon me that most certainly in that moment I would have pardoned whosoever had done me an injury; and if one should then have questioned me concerning any matter, I could only have said unto him 'Love,' with a countenance clothed in humble-ness. . . ."

"And when for the first time this beatitude was denied me, I became possessed with such grief that parting myself from others, I went into a lonely place to bathe the ground with most bitter tears: and when, by this heat of weeping, I was somewhat relieved, I betook myself to my chamber, where I could lament unheard. . . ."

Dante then recounts further visions of Love, in one of which Love said: "It is my will that thou compose certain things in rhyme, in the which thou shalt set forth how strong a mastership I have ob-tained over thee, through her; and how thou wast hers even from childhood." And he inserts odes and sonnets on which he makes comments; and he nar-rates sundry episodes, how he saw Beatrice at a wedding feast; how she grieved for the death of her father; how he had a presentiment of her death; and other episodes. And in the middle he puts a long digression on poetry. Then he takes up the thread again.

"But returning to the matter of my discourse. This excellent lady, of whom I spake in what hath gone before, came at last into such favour with all men, that when she passed anywhere folk ran to behold her; which thing was a deep joy to me: and when she drew near unto any, so much truth and

simpleness entered into his heart, that he dared
neither to lift his eyes nor to return her salutation:
and unto this, many who have felt it can bear witness. She went along crowned and clothed with
humility, showing no whit of pride in all that she
heard and saw: and when she had gone by, it was said
of many: 'This is not a woman, but one of the beautiful angels of Heaven,' and there were some that said:
'This is surely a miracle; blessed be the Lord, who
hath power to work thus marvelously.' I say, of
very sooth, that she showed herself so gentle and so
full of all perfection, that she bred in those who
looked upon her a soothing quiet beyond any speech;
neither could any look upon her without sighing
immediately. These things, and things yet more
wonderful, were brought to pass through her miraculous virtue." So he wrote a sonnet to express in
poetry what he had just said:

> Tanto gentile e tanto onesta pare
>   La donna mia, quand' ella altrui saluta,
>   Ch' ogni lingua divien tremando muta,
>   E gli occhi non ardiscon di guardare.
> Ella sen va, sentendosi laudare,
>   Benignamente d'umiltà vestuta;
>   E par che sia una cosa venuta
>   Di cielo in terra a miracol mostrare.
> Mostrasi si piacente a chi la mira,
>   Che dà per gli occhi una dolcezza al core,
>   Che intender non la può chi non la prova.
> E par che della sua labbia si muova
>   Uno spirto soave e pien d'amore,
>   Che va dicendo all'anima: sospira.

My lady looks so gentle and so pure
  When yielding salutation by the way,
  That the tongue trembles and has nought to say,
And the eyes, which fain would see, may not endure.
And still, amid the praise she hears secure,
  She walks with humbleness for her array;
  Seeming a creature sent from Heaven to stay
On earth, and show a miracle made sure.
She is so pleasant in the eyes of men
That through the sight the inmost heart doth gain
  A sweetness which needs proof to know it by:
And from between her lips there seems to move
A soothing spirit that is full of love,
  Saying forever to the soul, "O sigh!"

He also wrote another sonnet and began an ode
to tell of the manner in which he was subject to her
influence. Then he says: "I was still occupied with
this poem . . . when the Lord God of justice called
my most gracious lady unto Himself, that she might
be glorious under the banner of that blessed Queen
Mary, whose name had always a deep reverence in
the words of holy Beatrice."

Then follow certain episodes, somewhat apart from
the main matter of the story, the last of which,
however, leads up to the sonnet that begins:

Oltre la spera, che più larga gira,
  Passa il sospiro ch' esce del mio core:
  Intelligenza nuova, che l'Amore
  Piangendo mette in lui, pur su lo tira.

Beyond the sphere which spreads to widest space
  Now soars the sigh that my heart sends above:
  A new perception born of grieving Love
Guideth it upward the untrodden ways.

And he says: "After writing this sonnet, it was given unto me to behold a very wonderful vision; wherein I saw things which determined me that I would say nothing further of this most blessed one, until such time as I could discourse more worthily concerning her. And to this end I labour all I can; as she well knoweth. Wherefore if it be His pleasure through whom is the life of all things, that my life continue with me a few years, it is my hope that I shall yet write concerning her what hath not before been written of any woman. After the which, may it seem good unto Him who is the Master of Grace, that my spirit should go hence to behold the glory of its lady: to wit, of that blessed Beatrice who now gazeth continually on His countenance *qui est per omnia saecula benedictus*" (ROSSETTI's translation).

Here we find the glory of God gleaming upon the young prophet and leading him on. It is a story illumined more by the light of heaven than of earth. The poet takes his memories of Beatrice, the beautiful girl with whom he played as a child and saw at rare intervals in his adolescence, and arranges them in order, as if they were comments, around a number of his earliest poems, both sonnets and odes, so that the poems are strung like beads on the thread of his experience. And since, at the time of writing, after the death of Beatrice, he has plunged into the study of scholastic philosophy, he gives to all his memories a touch of allegory, and indicates darkly how, to the discerning mind, they embody deep truths concerning the turning of the soul to God. At the same time, possessed by a sense that the

mystery of Godhead is in all about us, he seeks to
indicate the presence of this mystery by recounting
his visions, real or imaginary, and by dwelling upon
mystic numbers, three, nine, and seven. No doubt,
the conscious artist is at work; and the whole
scheme of the book shows that Dante has been under
the influence of Guido Guinizelli's famous ode:

> Al cor gentil ripara sempre Amore
>   Siccome augello in selva alla verdura.
> Nè fe' Amore avanti gentil core,
>   Nè gentil core avanti Amor, Natura:

> Within the gentle heart Love shelters him,
>   As birds within the green shade of the grove.
> Before the gentle heart, in Nature's scheme,
>   Love was not, nor the gentle heart ere Love.

> D. G. ROSSETTI

For Dante human love, such love as his for Beatrice, is a ray of God's light; and this it is impossible
for the human tongue to describe. Nevertheless, by
means of poetry, theology, and philosophy, it may
be stammeringly hinted at; and this he did in the
Vita Nuova. As to the fashion and workmanship of
the little book, Dante makes use of familiar methods.
Visions of Love, the purifying power of his lady's
salutation, the idea of a "screen" lady, are all in
conventional use in Provençal and Italian poetry;
and, as I have said, the whole book is shaped and
colored by his youthful enthusiasm for lyric poetry
and scholastic philosophy, but still out of the
pages of this record of his new life shines the illumination of a soul that is radiant with light of the
revelation of God.

CHAPTER IV

AFTER THE DEATH OF BEATRICE

BEATRICE PORTINARI married Simone de' Bardi, a member of a great Florentine banking house, in 1287, and died in 1290. The *Vita Nuova* was probably written a year or two afterwards, as Dante was nearing thirty. During this early period of his manhood, covered by the narrative in the *Vita Nuova*, notwithstanding the great internal drama that centered around Beatrice, he led the ordinary life of a citizen of Florence of the educated upper class. His biographer, Leonardo Bruni (1369–1444), says: "He devoted himself not only to literature but to the other liberal studies, leaving nothing one side that is appropriate to make a man excel. Nor, for all this, did he shut himself up in an easy life, or keep himself apart from the world, but he lived and went about with other young men of his age, well-behaved, alert, and good at every manly exercise. So much so that in the great and memorable battle of Campaldino, a mere lad but well thought of, he took part on horseback in the front rank and fought vigorously, and ran into great danger. . . . After the battle Dante returned home and devoted himself to his studies more than ever,

but nevertheless he did not neglect the polite society
of the town. It is extraordinary that though he
studied continually, nobody would have thought
that he was a student, because of his gay manners
(*usanza lieta*)."

Of this *lieta usanza* we get a glimpse in the following sonnet to Guido Cavalcanti, the poet:

> Guido, vorrei che tu e Lapo ed io
>   Fossimo presi per incantamento,
>   E messi ad un vascel, ch' ad ogni vento
>   Per mare andasse a voler vostro e mio;
> Sicchè fortuna, od altro tempo rio
>   Non ci potesse dare impedimento,
>   Anzi, vivendo sempre in un talento,
>   Di stare insieme crescesse il disio.
> E Monna Vanna e Monna Lagia poi,
>   Con quella ch' è sul numero del trenta,
>   Con noi ponesse il buono incantatore:
> E quivi ragionar sempre d'amore;
>   E ciascuna di lor fosse contenta,
>   Siccome io credo che sariamo noi.

> Guido, I wish that Lapo,[1] thou, and I,
>   Could be by spells convey'd, as it were now,
>   Upon a barque, with all the winds that blow
> Across all seas at our good will to hie.
> So no mischance nor temper of the sky
>   Should mar our course with spite or cruel slip;
>   But we, observing old companionship,
> To be companions still should long thereby.
> And Lady Joan and Lady Lagia [2]

[1] Lapo Gianni, the poet.
[2] Rossetti wrote "Beatrice" following a reading of the
Italian text now no longer accepted.

And her the thirtieth [1] on my roll, with us
  Should our good wizard set, o'er seas to move
  And not to talk of anything but love:
And they three ever to be well at ease
  As we should be, I think, if this were thus.

D. G. ROSSETTI

Boccaccio says: "His mind and intelligence growing with his years, he did not turn to lucrative studies to which everybody hurries nowadays, but with a praiseworthy love of enduring fame he despised transitory riches and gave himself over to acquire complete knowledge of poetry and of the poetic art. In the course of this he became very familiar with Virgil, Horace, Ovid, Statius, and every other famous poet; he not only took pains to know them, but by writing poetry in an elevated style he strove to imitate them, as his works show."

His works show that he not only studied poetry, but all books of philosophy and learning that he could lay hands on: volumes of Aristotle that had been translated into Latin, such bits of Plato as were accessible, scraps of Homer, certain works of Cicero, Seneca, and Boethius, treatises that came from the Arabic through the Moors, St. Augustine, Albertus Magnus, and Thomas Aquinas. He began his studies while quite young. He says, quoting Aristotle: "All men by nature desire to know," and no doubt after the death of Beatrice, in order to distract his mind, he took to study with far greater zeal.

---

[1] This number, "thirtieth," seems to be the "Screen Lady."

There is one episode concerning his life related in the latter part of the *Vita Nuova*, which, if we accept Dante's subsequent explanation of it, bears upon the matter of his studies at this time; his explanation also raises the whole question of his use of allegory, and as this is necessary to an understanding of the *Commedia*, it is worth while to pause over it. He tells how, a year after Beatrice's death, he was standing, with all his sorrow depicted in his face, and says: "I lifted mine eyes to look; and then perceived a young and very beautiful lady, who was gazing upon me from a window with a gaze full of pity, so that the very sum of pity appeared gathered together in her. . . . It happened after this, that whensoever I was seen of this lady, she became pale and of a piteous countenance, as though it had been with love; whereby she remembered me many times of my own most noble lady, who was wont to be of a like paleness. And I know that often, when I could not weep nor in any way give ease unto mine anguish, I went to look upon this lady, who seemed to bring the tears into my eyes by the mere sight of her. . . . At length, by the constant sight of this lady, mine eyes began to be gladdened overmuch with her company; through which thing many times I had much unrest, and rebuked myself as a base person." And a little further on he says: "The sight of this lady brought me into so unwonted a condition that I often thought of her as of one too dear unto me; and I began to consider her thus: 'This lady is young, beautiful, gentle, and wise: perchance it was Love himself who set her in my path, that so my life might find peace.' And there were times when I thought yet more fondly, until my heart consented unto its reasoning" (D. G. ROSSETTI).

There can be little doubt that this episode is literally true, and that Dante, as a relief from sorrow, turned toward this gentle Lady of the Window, and transferred some, at least, of his devotion from Beatrice to her. Afterwards, it seems, he was blamed by his friends and acquaintances for levity and inconstancy; and, in the *Convivio*, he boldly asserts that the Lady of the Window is mere allegory, and that he meant by her nothing but Philosophy. It is very hard for modern readers to accept this explanation; it looks as if Dante's love, and perhaps his pride, had revolted at his own inconstancy, and that he had succeeded in persuading himself, and sought to persuade his friends, that he had not really fallen in love with another woman.

But in judging human conduct we are dealing with subtle mysteries of motives, impulses, feelings, thoughts that shift, meet, combine, and separate like clouds; and it may be that Dante had begun to fix his thoughts so much more upon the divine symbolism in Beatrice than upon her earthly person that he had really transferred all his thoughts to that allegorical plane, and that at the period of his writing the gentle Lady of the Window had undergone a similar transformation. In those times almost everything, especially where the deeper emotions were concerned, was interpreted as the literal expression of some spiritual reality. To-day we are far removed from that theory; nevertheless, life as it

reveals itself has too many "shoots of everlasting-
ness" for the human heart to accept the reports of
our senses as literally true. Only the hard-and-fast
materialist accepts the sensual presentation of the
external world as true and final. Most of us look
upon the literal presentation of life with a reserva-
tion and bow our heads before the mystery.

Dante was convinced that he was always confronted by an allegory. "The things which are seen
are temporal, but the things which are not seen are
eternal" (II Cor. iv, 18). All thoughtful men of the
Middle Ages accepted life as a parable, and bestirred
themselves to find out the meaning behind the veil.
Theologians employed this method in the interpretation of Holy Writ; St. Paul did so, and so do all
interpreters from St. Paul to Swedenborg, and from
Swedenborg until to-day. In Dante's time the same
method was employed in interpreting the classical
poets. Boccaccio expresses the common view:
"Holy Writ, which we call theology, sometimes under the figure of a story, sometimes under that of
a vision, sometimes under the guise of lamentation,
or in many another way, means to show us the deep
mystery about the incarnation of the Word, His life,
the things that happened at His death, His triumphant resurrection, His miraculous ascension, and
about everything He did. . . . So, poets in their
works, which we call poetry, by the fiction of different
gods, by the metamorphosis of men into idle shapes,
and sometimes by light-minded discoursing, have
shown us the causes of things, the consequences of
virtues and vices, what we ought to shun and what

to follow, so that at the last we may come, by doing
what is right, to that goal which they [the pagan
poets] who did not rightly know the true God believed to be the height of salvation."

Dante also, in his famous letter to Can Grande
della Scala, lord of Verona, which serves as a preface
to the *Commedia*, sets forth the method of allegorical
explanation, and gives this example of the different
ways of interpreting a verse from the Bible: "'When
Israel went out of Egypt, the House of Jacob from
a people of strange language, Judah was his sanc-
tuary and Israel his dominion' (Psalm cxiv, 1–2).
Should we consider the *letter* only, the exit of the
Children of Israel from Egypt in the time of Moses,
is what is signified to us; if the *allegory*, our redemption through Christ is signified to us; if the *moral*
sense, the conversion of the mind from the grief
and misery of sin to the state of grace is signified
to us; if the *anagogical*, the exit of the holy soul
from the slavery of this corruption to the liberty of
eternal glory is signified. And although these mystic
senses are called by various names they may all
in general be called allegorical, since they differ
from the literal or historical."

This mode of interpretation, that appears so
fantastic to us, was to the men of that time as
familiar and natural as any of our rules of deduction
sanctioned by logic. Dante applied this method, not
as an artist, but unconsciously in all good faith to
Beatrice Portinari and to the gentle Lady of the
Window. Literally they were two lovely maidens;
allegorically they could easily become Theology and

Philosophy. So, when Dante explains to us that the second lady is in fact Philosophy, he may in very truth have dropped from his mind her perishable part and be concerned solely with her spiritual significance. At least, he says so himself: "I, who was seeking to console myself, found not only a cure for my tears, but words of authors, and of sciences, and of books, pondering upon which I judged that Philosophy, who was the lady of these authors, of these sciences, and of these books, was a thing supreme; and I conceived her after the fashion of a gentle lady, and I might not conceive her in any attitude save that of compassion; wherefore the sense for truth so loved to gaze upon her that I could scarce turn it away from her; and impelled by this imagination of her, I began to go where she was in very truth revealed, to wit, to the schools of the religious orders, and to the disputations of the philosophers; so that in a short time, I suppose some thirty months, I began to feel so much of her sweetness that the love of her expelled and destroyed every other thought" (*Conv.* II, ch. 13).

It may be that Dante, under the influence of his studies and his pride, has distorted the natural, literal interpretation of the Lady of the Window, or, it may be that the original passage in the *Vita Nuova* is allegorical; in either view the episode helps us to realize how completely the habit of accepting life as a mere colored veil concealing the reality behind had possession of Dante, and thereby helps us to understand the *Commedia*.

But, whether or no his attentions to the Lady of

the Window were tinged with disloyalty to Beatrice,
some far more serious infidelity to her memory took
place in these years. Just what this falling away
from her ideals was, we can only infer from what he
and others say; but it was black enough to give him
the bitter, poignant consciousness of sin that is
shown in the *Inferno*. It seems most likely that
(apart from the pervading sin of pride) Dante was

> nel diletto della carne involto,

> in the pleasures of the flesh enmeshed.

The testimony to this sin is very strong. Guido
Cavalcanti, in a sonnet to Dante, applies the words
"base" and "abject" to Dante's way of life. Boccaccio says: "With such great virtue, with so much
learning, as has been shown to belong to this wondrous poet, sensuality found too great a place, not
only in his youthful years but also in his maturity."
And, at this period of his life, Forese Donati, a glut-
tonous, dissolute fellow (*Purg.* XXIII), was his
boon companion. There still exist half a dozen
ribald sonnets, in which the two friends revile one
another for discreditable conduct in a very unedi-
fying manner. And — though at a later period —
Dante also wrote several odes to a young woman
with a heart, he says, as hard as stone, but who
is very beautiful:

> Quand' ella ha in testa una ghirlanda d'erba,
> trae della mente nostra ogni altra donna;
> perchè si mischia il crespo giallo e'l verde
> sì bel, ch' Amor vi viene a stare all' ombra.

When on her head she wears a garland wrought of leaves
She draws from out my mind all women else;
The green so sweetly mingles with her golden locks,
That Love himself would nestle in their shade.

[Canzone I]

These odes express a love quite other than that
which he felt for Beatrice. In addition to all this,
in the *Purgatorio*, after he has ascended to the top
of the Mount of Purgatory, Dante is obliged to pass
through the fire that hedges off the Earthly Paradise
from the last circle of Purgatory, and also, it seems,
purifies sins of the flesh. It is obvious that this narrative reveals an inner drama.

After he has passed the fire and stands in the
presence of Beatrice, he feels himself dissolve in
shame. She rebukes him, before a multitude of holy
spirits, sternly almost cruelly, so that his sorrow
shall equal his sin (*Purg.* XXX, 108), and says:

Questi fu tal nella sua vita nuova
    virtualmente, ch' ogni abito destro
    fatto avrebbe in lui mirabil prova.
Ma tanto più maligno e più silvestro
    si fa il terren col mal seme e non colto,
    quant' egli ha più del buon vigor terrestro.
Alcun tempo il sostenni col mio volto;
    mostrando gli occhi giovinetti a lui,
    meco il menava in dritta parte volto.
Sì tosto come in su la soglia fui
    di mia seconda etade, e mutai vita,
    questi si tolse a me, a diessi altrui.
Quando di carne a spirto era salita,
    e bellezza e virtù cresciuta m' era,
    fu' io a lui men cara e men gradita;
e volse i passi suoi per via non vera,
    imagini di ben seguendo false,
    che nulla promission rendono intera.

Nè impetrare spirazion mi valse,
    con le quali ed in sogno ed altrimenti
    lo rivocai; sì poco a lui ne calse.
Tanto giù cadde, che tutti argomenti
    alla salute sua eran già corti,
    fuor che mostrargli le perdute genti.
Per questo visitai l'uscio dei morti,
    ed a colui che l'ha quassù condotto
    li preghi miei, piangendo, furon porti.
Alto fato di Dio sarebbe rotto,
    se Lete si passasse, e tal vivanda
    fosse gustata senza alcuno scotto
di pentimento che lagrime spanda.

This man in his New Life was able to be such
    That every beneficial aptitude
    Would have wrought wonderful effects in him.
But so much the more malignant and more wild
    The ground becomes with evil seeded, and unplowed,
    According as it has more vigorous soil.
Awhile I, by my presence, held him up;
    And looking on him with my maiden eyes
    I took him with me turned to righteousness.
But soon as I had reached a later time
    Of womanhood and quitted mortal life,
    Me he forsook and unto others turned.
When I from flesh to spirit had uprisen
    With both my beauty and my worth increased,
    To him I was less pleasing and less dear;
He bent his footsteps by a path not true,
    To chase deceitful images of good
    That never keep their promise honestly.
Nor did the spiritual help I gave
    Avail, with which in dreams and other ways
    I called him back; so little did he heed.
He fell so low, that all the arguments for
    His salvation's sake were found too scant,
    Except the sight of the lost souls in hell.

Therefore, I sought the threshold of the dead,
  And weeping made petition unto him
  Who has conducted this man up to here.
The high decree of God would broken be
  If Lethe he should cross and taste our fruit,
  And pay no penitential scot of tears.

                    Purg. XXX, 115–145

Dante admits that all she says is true and bursts
into a torrent of tears; and she goes on:

        Per entro i miei disiri,
  che ti menavano ad amar lo bene
  di là dal qual non è a che s' aspiri,
quai fossi attraversati o quai catene
  trovasti, per che del passare innanzi
  dovessiti così spogliar la spene?
E quali agevolezze o quali avanzi
  nella fronte degli altri si mostraro,
  per che dovessi lor passeggiare anzi?

        Within your yearnings up toward me,
  That then were leading you to love the good
  Which is the final goal to be aspired to,
What pitfalls in your way, what chains
  Found you? that made you lay aside your hope
  Of going on; or what sweet winsomeness
Or promises upon the brow of others were there shown
  That you to meet them needs must take your way?

                    Purg. XXXI, 22–30

Dante, still weeping, replies:

        Le presenti cose
  col falso lor piacer volser miei passi,
  tosto che il vostro viso si nascose.

        Immediate things
  With their deceitful pleasures turned my steps
  Aside, soon as your face was hid.

                    Ib. 34–37

Beatrice grants that confession and repentance mitigate the sin, but bids him stop weeping and listen to her rebuke:

> perchè altra volta
> udendo le Sirene sie più forte

> so that another time
> Hearing the Sirens thou mayest be more strong.

Ib. 44–45

Then she says, — and the reader must remember that she has been transmuted into Divine Wisdom:

> Mai non t' appresentò natura o arte
>   piacer, quanto le belle membra in ch' io
>   rinchiusa fui, e sono in terra sparte;
> e se il sommo piacer sì ti fallio
>   per la mia morte, qual cosa mortale
>   dovea poi trarre te nel suo disio?
> Ben ti dovevi, per lo primo strale
>   delle cose fallaci, levar suso
>   di retro a me che non era più tale.
> Non ti dovean gravar le penne in giuso,
>   ad aspettar più colpi, o pargoletta,
>   o altra vanità con sì breve uso.

> Never did nature, nor did art, to you
>   Pleasure present, so great as the fair limbs
>   In which I was enclosed, and now are one with earth;
> And when this greatest pleasure by my death
>   Came to an end, what mortal thing
>   Ought then to lure you by a love of it?
> Rather you should, at the first arrow of
>   Deceitful things, have mounted upward after me
>   Who was no longer of their world.
> No girl, nor vain thing else (so quick to pass)
>   Should have been able to weigh down your wings,
>   To wait for further shots.

Ib. 49–60

In these verses not only does Divine Wisdom rebuke human frailty but also Beatrice, the woman,
rebukes her erring lover; and the reproof strengthens
the hypothesis that Dante had been false to a human,
as well as to a divine, loyalty. But Beatrice's last
words *altra vanilà* (1. 60) indicate other failings; and
this, too, is vaguely confirmed by her further words:

> e veggi vostra via dalla divina
>   distar cotanto, quanto si discorda
>   da terra il ciel che più alto festina.

> And see, your way is distant from the way
>   Divine as far, as is the highest heaven
>   That whirls above distant from earth.

Ib. XXXIII, 88–90

Therefore, according to Beatrice, Dante's path had
led him directly away from God, into the region
where God is not, which is sin, although she gives
no hint of its nature. All this is autobiographical, and
will help us to understand Dante's bitter consciousness of sin, and the whole scheme of the *Commedia*.

CHAPTER V

EXILE

OF outward events in Dante's life after he wrote the *Vita Nuova*, we know little. He married a Florentine lady, Gemma Donati, and had four children, two boys and two girls. He took part in the public affairs of the city, and became a member of the more important councils. He qualified himself for office, as was necessary under a recent democratic law, by enrolling in a guild; as he had neither a profession nor a trade, he chose the guild of Physicians and Apothecaries, to which it seems men of letters and artists naturally turned. In the year 1300 he was elected one of the six priors, a board which constituted the supreme executive body in the state. "All the ills and misfortunes that befell me," he wrote, "had their cause and origin in the unlucky sessions of my priorate" (Bruni). It was a tumultuous time in Florence; political passions rose to fighting heat, and the two parties that divided the city, known as the Neri (Blacks) and the Bianchi (Whites), came to blows. The priors, trying to act with impartiality, banished the chiefs of both factions. One of these was Dante's particular friend, Guido Cavalcanti, of the Bianchi faction. But the efforts of the

priors to establish peace, with justice to both parties,
were in vain; outside powers, too mighty to be
resisted, tipped the scales. Pope Boniface VIII,
scheming to get the city in his clutches, made an
unscrupulous bargain with the Neri, and sent a
blackguardly French prince, Charles of Valois, with
a body of men-at-arms, to do what he called bringing about peace and order. Prince Charles promptly
put the Neri in power; and they, with equal prompti-
tude, treated Florence like a conquered city and
proscribed the principal men of the Bianchi faction.
Dante's patriotic opposition to the Pope had marked
him for vengeance; he was summoned to trial on
trumped-up charges of corruption and of actions
hostile to the Pope, as if his duty had been to the
Pope and not to his city. He did not obey the sum-
mons, and was condemned to exile for two years, to
disfranchisement and to a fine, and if the fine were
not paid within three days, then to the forfeiture of
all his property. A second decree, six weeks later,
condemned him to be burned alive (January and
March, 1300).

So, leading the life of the world brought Dante to
his worldly undoing. Banished from home, his property confiscated, condemned to leave his wife, his
little children, his friends, the beautiful city of his
youth and of his forefathers, which he loved so
passionately, and to roam poor, despised, begging
alms at the courts of princes, — this, as the world
judges, was the very failure of failures. The passages
in which he speaks of his exile are fraught with
pathos:

Tu lascerai ogni cosa diletta
   più caramente, e questo è quello strale
   che l'arco dello esilio pria saetta.
Tu proverai sì come sa di sale
   lo pane altrui, e com' è duro calle
   lo scendere e il salir per l'altrui scale.

Thou shalt leave everything most dearly loved;
   This is the dart, the bow of exile first shall shoot.
And thou shalt prove how salt the taste
   Of others' bread, and what a rugged path
   Descending and ascending others' stairs.

Par. XVII, 55–60

And in the *Convivio* he says:

"Since it was the pleasure of the citizens of the
most beauteous and the most famous daughter of
Rome, Florence, to cast me forth from her most
sweet bosom (wherein I was born and nurtured until
the culmination of my life, wherein with their good
leave I long with all my heart to repose my wearied
mind and end the time which is granted me), through
well-nigh all the regions whereto this tongue [the
Italian language] extends, a wanderer, almost a
beggar, have I paced, revealing, against my will, the
wound of fortune, which is often wont to be unjustly
imputed to him who is wounded. Verily have I been
a ship without sail and without helm, drifted upon
divers ports and straits and shores by the dry wind
that grievous poverty exhales" (First Treatise, ch.
III, Temple Classics).

Dante did not know, he could not know, as he
drifted like a hulk over that tempestuous sea, that,
next to Beatrice exile would be his truest guide to

help him reach the "glorious haven" that Brunetto
Latini had foreseen for him. Exile detached his
heart from vanities that had assailed his attention
and held it in servitude. Exile taught him the difference between things that pass and things that abide;
exile turned his thoughts from the outward world
in upon himself. He learned, as few have learned,
how

> The mind is its own place and in itself
> Can make a heaven of hell, a hell of heaven.

In exile, as he wandered about, he learned that the
confusion in Florence was matched by the confusion
in all Italy; but he also learned that the bitterness
in political confusion is due not to the tumult that
rages without, but to the shaken equilibrium of the
soul within. In exile he acquired the painful knowledge that he himself had wrought the disorder in his
own heart, in that, captivated by the false glitter of
appearances, he had followed paths that lead away
from God; but he acquired also the comforting
knowledge that in his heart he could find shelter
from all disorder, the peace that the world cannot
give, the truth that the Kingdom of Heaven is
within us. This is the deep doctrine that lies at the
heart of Christianity.

There are various ways of finding the hidden God
within. St. John of the Cross teaches us one way:
"God abides in the very innermost depths of the
soul, and there He hides. So the soul that would find
Him must issue forth by means of affection and of
will from all that is created, and enter into herself
in a musing so profound that all creation becomes

for her as if it were not. That is why St. Augustine says: 'I despatched my outward senses, as scouts, to seek Thee, but I did not find Thee, for I sought unwisely. For now I see, God, my light, that hast enlightened me, that I sought Thee unwisely by my scouts, because Thou art within me.' So, indeed, God is hidden in the soul, and therein must the repentant, in contemplation, seek it with love, crying 'Where art Thou hid?'" (*Canticle of the Spirit*).

And Meister Eckhardt has his way, which he tells in this dialogue:

Qu. What sort of man are you?
Ans. I am a king.
Qu. Where is your kingdom?
Ans. My soul is my kingdom, for I can so rule my senses inward and outward that all the desires and powers of my soul are in subjection, and this kingdom is greater than a kingdom on earth.
Qu. What brought you to this perfection?
Ans. My silence, my high thoughts, and my union with God. For I could not rest in anything that was less than God. Now I have found God; and in God have eternal rest and peace.[1]

Others attain to this knowledge by voluntary renunciation, by vows of chastity and obedience, by giving up ambition and all the things of this world. But the ways of contemplation, of voluntary poverty, of renunciation were not ways natural to the proud aristocrat Dante. Some other way had to be opened to him. Exile for him was, next to Beatrice, the highest manifestation of God's grace. Had it not been for exile, Dante would not have learned

[1] Quoted in *Mysticism*, by Evelyn Underhill, p. 253.

that the Kingdom of Heaven is within, and would have floundered about seeking for the highest good in a return to Florence and a laurel crown in the Baptistery of San Giovanni, and the *Divine Comedy* would not have been written. He wandered in many places suffering contumely; but he perceived at last that the drama of Emperor and Pope, of rival barons, of proud cities, was but as a play of shadows cast upon a screen compared with the drama in the depths of his own soul.

As to where Dante wandered to, there are some scanty records, scattered about in archives, that prove Dante to have been in one or two places on such and such a date; and there are in the *Commedia* many descriptions of places and allusions to persons which enable the painstaking student to follow Dante's footsteps in at least a part of his wanderings. At first he joined a company of exiles, most of whom belonged to the old aristocratic Ghibelline faction that had been expelled from Florence thirty or forty years before, and with them he plotted to return by force of arms; but the attempt failed, and Dante, disgusted with his associates, went his own way alone. He found refuge and hospitality in Verona, at the court of the della Scala; later he became the guest of the Malaspina family, in the northwest of Tuscany. Afterwards he went to the upper waters of the Arno, to Bologna, to Lucca, and elsewhere, in different parts of Lombardy and Tuscany.

All the time he nursed his passionate longing to return to Florence, and his hopes rose high several times. At one period he thought that the governors

of the city would have a change of heart, and he
wrote letters to various citizens to use their influence on his behalf, but all in vain. Then suddenly
hope flared up like a bonfire. For over fifty years no
Emperor had come to Italy. Rudolph of Hapsburg
(1273–1291) and his successors had concerned themselves only with German affairs and their own for-
tunes; but in 1308 a new Emperor was elected,
Henry VII, who proclaimed that he would not neglect
his duty to Italy as his predecessors had done; and
after his coronation Henry announced his intention
of crossing the Alps and of coming to Italy. Dante
was almost beside himself. He wrote exultingly one
of his strange, mediaeval letters, directed to the
Princes of Italy: "Lo, now is the acceptable time
wherein arise the signs of consolation and peace.
For a new day beginneth to glow, showing forth the
dawn which is even now dissipating the darkness of
our long calamity; and already the breezes of the
east begin to blow, the lips of heaven glow red, and
confirm the auspices of the nations with a caressing
calm. And we, too, shall see the looked-for joy, we
who have kept vigil through the long night in the
desert. For peace-bringing Titan shall arise, and
Justice . . . will revive again so soon as he shall
brandish his first ray. All they who hunger and
thirst shall be satisfied in the light of his rays, and
they who love iniquity shall be confounded before
his shining face. For the strong lion of the tribe
of Judah [Christ] hath lifted up his merciful ears,
and, taking pity on the wail of universal captivity,
hath raised up a second Moses to snatch his people

from the burdens of the Egyptians, leading them
to a land that floweth with milk and honey. . . .
Awake then all ye dwellers in Italy and arise before
your king since ye are destined not only to obey his
command, but, as free-born children, to follow his
guidance" (Epistola V, Temple Classics).

But the Guelfs of Italy did not hearken to Dante;
they stood apart, hostile, and the city of Florence
put herself at the head of the opposition. At this,
Dante wrote a letter of warning to the Florentines;
but they took no notice of him; on the contrary, they
strengthened their fortifications and prepared for defense. Then Dante, in a fury, wrote to the Emperor
(who, in Dante's view, was wasting his strength
against minor enemies in Lombardy), a fiery letter
in which he denounced the city and its leaders:

"Dost thou not know, most excellent of princes,
and from the watch tower of highest exaltation dost
thou not perceive where the fox of this stench skulks
in safety from the hunters? For the culprit drinketh
not of the headlong Po, nor of thy Tiber, but her
jaws do ever pollute the streams of the torrent of
Arno; and (knowest thou not perchance?) this dire
plague is named Florence. She is the viper that turns
upon the entrails of her mother. She is the sick sheep
that infects the flock of her lord with her contagion.
. . . In truth, with the fierceness of a viper she is
striving to rend her mother, for she hath sharpened
the horns of rebellion against Rome, who created her
in her image and after her likeness" (Epistola VII,
Temple Classics).

Henry VII did his best. He strove gallantly to restore the power of the Empire in Italy, but he was striving to restore what Time had abolished; his peaceful efforts, and his warlike efforts were alike unavailing. He marched here and there, and laid siege to Florence, but all in vain. Suddenly he fell ill of a fever and died, and with him perished the last hope of bringing the Holy Roman Empire back to life, and Dante's last hope of returning to Florence by means of force.

An opportunity of recall, however, was offered to him. Exiles such as he were granted a pardon upon condition that they should pay a fine and present themselves according to the usage prescribed for pardoned criminals, before the altar in the Baptistery, confess their wrongdoing and abase themselves. Some kinsman, a priest apparently, wrote him of this ungenerous offer of clemency. We have Dante's letter in reply: "With grateful mind and close attention did I perceive from your letter, received with due reverence and affection, how deeply you have my recall at heart. And thereby you have bound me under the closer obligation because it so rarely chanceth that exiles find friends. But I go on to answer the contents of it. And if my answer be not such as perchance the pusillanimity of certain might seek, I would beg you, in all affection, to winnow it in your judgment before you pronounce upon it.

"This, then, is what has been indicated to me by the letters of your nephew and mine, and many other friends, as to the decree recently passed in Florence concerning the pardon of the exiles: That if I will consent to pay a certain sum of money, and be willing to bear the brand of oblation, I may be absolved and may return at once. Wherein are two things ridiculous and ill-advised, O father! I say ill-advised by those who have expressed them; for your letter, more discreetly and advisedly drawn up, contained no hint of them.

"Is this the glorious recall whereby Dante Alighieri is summoned back to his country after suffering well-nigh fifteen years of exile? Is this the reward of innocence manifest to all the world, of unbroken sweat and toil in study? Far be it from the disciple of philosophy, this abject-self-abasement of a soul of clay! To allow himself to be presented at the altar, as a prisoner after the fashion of . . . some infamous wretch. Far be it from the preacher of justice, when he hath suffered a wrong, to pay his coin to them that inflicted it as though they had deserved well of him.

"Not this the way of return to my country, O my father! But if another may hereafter be found by you or any other, which hurts not Dante's fair fame and honour, that will I accept with no lagging feet. If no such path leads back to Florence, then will I never enter Florence more. What then? May I not gaze upon the mirror of the sun and stars wherever I may be? Can I not ponder on the sweetest truths wherever I may be beneath the heaven, but I must first make me inglorious, nay infamous, before the people and the state of Florence? Nor shall I lack for bread" (Epistola IX, Temple Classics).

There is another reference to his exile contained in what is known as Fra Ilario's letter. This letter has usually been considered a forgery; and it certainly contains matter that seems a jumble of errors. Nevertheless it goes back to the time of Boccaccio, and, at least in this one passage, gives what might well have been an account of a real meeting between a friar on a remote mountain and this lonely wanderer. The writer describes a visit of Dante's to his monastery in the Apennines: "Hither he came, passing through the diocese of Luni, moved either by the religion of the place or by some other feeling. And seeing him as yet unknown to me and to all my brethren, I questioned him of his wishings and his seekings there. He moved not; but stood silently contemplating the columns and arches of the cloister. And again I asked him what he wished and whom he sought. Then, slowly turning his head, and looking at the friars and at me, he answered 'Peace!'" (LONGFELLOW's *Illustrations*, etc.).

So he wandered on, the proud, lonely, passionate man. He could not tell that the seeds which Beatrice had sown in his heart depended upon loneliness, bitterness of soul, and degradation in the eyes of men, for their ripening. Or did he, with the confidence of genius that resists and overcomes all the buffetings of adverse circumstances, feel assured that, come good, come ill, in either event he should prove his soul, and write concerning Beatrice "what had not before been written of any woman"? In his letter to the Princes of Italy he said: "It is not always we who act. Nay sometimes we are God's instruments, and human wills, which are by nature free, are sometimes driven without touch of lower affection, submissive to the eternal will, serving it often though they know it not" (Epistola V).

During these years, chiefly (it seems) during the last ten years of his life, following Beatrice as a star, and taught in the school of Exile, Dante composed the *Commedia*, the great poem upon which later generations have conferred the epithet *Divine*.

CHAPTER VI

INTELLECTUAL PREPARATION

BEATRICE was the guiding star that directed Dante towards God, and Exile was the cruel yet kindly power that detached him from false values of life. Beatrice was to him what the Church is to the devout Catholic, what the Bible is to the strict Protestant, a light emanating from the True Light that lighteth the world. Exile was to him what Poverty was to St. Francis of Assisi, not merely detachment from riches, luxury, material possessions, but a spiritual freedom; it unbound the cords that tied him to the world, it freed his soul from the hindrances of lesser desires. Both Beatrice and Exile were vouchsafed to him, as it were, by the grace of God, that he might be able to attain his full spiritual stature and strength, and reveal to men, in the appropriate language of noblest poetry, his conviction of what is worthy and what is worthless in this strange and wonderful human pilgrimage from the dark to the dark.

But Dante was no passive instrument in the hands of fate; he was aware of his own genius, he comprehended the magnitude of the task that he was undertaking, and prepared himself as best he could to execute it. He had started upon the quest of God, and though in the end he found that he must look for God within his own heart, in the beginning he thought that he must look for Him in the outside universe, believing that the way of the intellect was the true road, because, as he judged, if one has eyes to see, God reveals Himself in all objects of sense, in all the workings of the universe. So Dante set out to master all knowledge. Even in his youth, as we learn from the *Vita Nuova*, he had begun with diligence, and as years went on he devoted to his task what time was not taken up by the immediate demands of life. He studied when and where he could, and became one of the most learned men of his generation, if not actually the most learned of all. To his contemporaries his renown as a man of learning was almost as great as his renown as a poet. The historian Giovanni Villani (a contemporary) wrote: "Dante was very well read in almost every science, although he was a layman; he was a very great poet and philosopher and a perfect master of style"; and from what he says concerning the *Divine Comedy*, it appears that he was more impressed by the subtle discussions in it upon ethics, natural history, astrology, philosophy, and theology, than by its poetry. The same opinion prevailed in the next generation. Antonio Pucci, a Florentine poet, depicts the seven liberal arts, Grammar, Logic, Rhetoric, Arithmetic, Geometry, Music, and Astronomy, as weeping and tearing their hair at Dante's death, while Theology tries to console them; but he says nothing of the Muses. No witnesses, however, outside of Dante's writings are needed to prove his learning.

His writings are stuffed with references and quotations. In this stage of study and self-preparation, certain particular matters, at one period and another, came to the front and occupied his attention, in especial the Italian language, philosophy, and politics, upon each of which he wrote a book.

The treatise on the Italian language, *De Vulgari Eloquentia*, written in Latin, is a book of remarkable scholarship for the time. Italian, in her development from the Latin, had lingered behind her sister tongues of France, Provence, and Spain. The reasons for this are easily understood. In Italy the Latin language naturally had a more tenacious hold than elsewhere in Europe, and had received a smaller admixture of foreign words; therefore Italian had been tardier in growing out of the debased Latin of the dark ages into a modern language. And even after what may be called Italian had become the common speech of the people, it found Latin entrenched across its path, thwarting its progress towards becoming the accepted mode of expression either in writing or talking for educated men. Latin was the language of the Church, of the law, of government, of all serious affairs; it was taught in the schools as the language of the upper class; it held a large place in the patriotic heart, for it was all that was left of the imperial inheritance from ancient Rome, mistress of the world. The Italians proudly called it "*la lingua nostra latina*" — "our Latin language." So that in the twelfth century, although there were already national literatures in England, Germany, France, Provence, and Spain, there was none in

Italy. The earliest specimen of Italian poetry that
has any interest for modern readers is St. Francis's
canticle to the sun. But that canticle is outside the
main channel of Italian poetry. That main channel
takes us back to Provence.

Provençal poetry had at this time already reached
a high stage of delicate lyrical finish; it was conventional, refined, aristocratic, fit for the leisure
of pleasure-loving lords and ladies. Troubadours
wandered into Italy; and so great was the prestige of
Provençal poetry in Lombardy that many poets,
Italian born, wrote their lyrics in Provençal and
in accordance with the rules of Provencal verse. Of
these the most famous is Sordello of Mantua, who
was still living, a man of more than three score,
when Dante was born. After the French crusaders,
led by Simon de Montfort and blessed by Pope
Innocent III, had trampled under foot the easy
pleasant civilization of Provence, many more troubadours sought refuge in Italy. So, of their own free
will or chased from home by invaders, Provençal
poets familiarly frequented the princely courts of
Italy.

From this Provençal poetry Italian lyrical poetry
took its origin. The earliest school had its home in
Southern Italy, and was called the Sicilian School,
although its members came from all about, because
its most distinguished patron, the Emperor Frederick II, was King of Sicily; its principal poets were
the Emperor himself, his two charming sons, Man-
fred and Enzio, his chief counselor, Pier della Vigna,
and Jacopo da Lentino, known from his profession as

the Notary, who, though the least of the group as a personage, was the most important as a poet. The next school in Italian poetry centers about Guitone of Arezzo (a little town in Tuscany near Florence), who lived till Dante was nearly thirty, and, as he seems to have spent the end of his life in Florence, may have been known to Dante. Then, for the third stage, the genius of poetry going north tarried in Bologna, where the great figure is Guido Guinizelli (1230?–1276), whom Dante admired greatly. In the *Purgatorio* Dante calls him

> il padre
> mio, e degli altri miei miglior, che mai
> rime d'amore usar dolci e leggiadre.

> My father,
> And of those, my betters, who ĕver made
> Sweet, gracious, dainty rhymes of love.

Purg. XXVI, 97–99

These earlier Italian poets imitated very closely their Provençal masters; but Guinizelli introduced an idealistic philosophy and a new manner into his poems, so that they became the starting point of a new Tuscan school, composed of Guido Cavalcanti, Dante, Cino of Pistoia, and others.

Provençal poetry and this early Italian poetry, Dante studied with great care. He had made his vow that he "would say nothing further of this most blessed one [Beatrice] until such time as he could discourse more worthily concerning her." And to be able to discourse worthily, he must become a master of the art of language. How diligently he investigated this art, the *De Vulgari Eloquentia* tells us. It is an admirable treatise, clear, learned, and scientific. Dante speaks of the origin of language, of its three great branches, and of the three subdivisions into which the branch prevailing in southwestern Europe was divided, the tongues in which yes is expressed by *oc*, *oïl*, and *sì*. He then sets out to see if there is an Italian language worthy to be the national, literary language, and in this quest examines and criticizes the numerous dialects of Italy. He enumerates them one by one and finds them all inadequate, and concludes that the Italian language he is looking for, worthy to serve the highest uses of educated men, is the general speech of all Italy freed from the peculiarities and grossness of local dialects. To this he applies the adjectives "illustrious, cardinal, courtly and curial," which means proper for palaces, courts of justice, and in general dignified and polished use. He then treats of this national literary language, of its employment in poetry, — especially for dealing with the proper subjects of lyrical poetry, war, love, and righteousness, — and more particularly in the ode (canzone). He analyzes and judges the structure of the ode, the number of syllables in the line, the words proper to be used, in short what we call the technique of the poetic art. The treatise was broken off abruptly, but there is enough to show that he took the greatest pains to master his art, so that the manner of his poem should be worthy of its matter.

The Banquet, *Il Convivio*, is a book, in Italian, on philosophy. In form it is a collection of his odes with

long glosses that are packed full of all the learning
of the time. In these glosses Dante takes the doctrines of the two great religious philosophers, Albertus Magnus and Thomas Aquinas, whose special
task had been to combine and reconcile the teachings
of Aristotle and of the Bible, and puts their doctrines
into a form more intelligible to persons who are not
scholars. The whole book is divided into parts, called
treatises, each treatise being a commentary on an
ode; of these there were to be fifteen, but only four
were completed. The first is introductory and sets
forth Dante's reasons for writing the book and for
writing it in Italian, instead of in Latin, which would
be the appropriate language for a work on philosophy.
In the second, he comments upon the ode that begins
with an apostrophe to the angelic beings who preside
over the heaven of Venus, from whence rain down
influences of love. The first line is,

Voi che intendendo il terzo ciel movete,

Ye who by understanding move the third heaven.

It is in this commentary that he states that by the
gentle Lady in the Window, spoken of in the *Vita
Nuova*, he represented Philosophy. Then, comment-
ing upon the verses in order, he adds an exposition
of the heavens, of the angelic intelligences that
govern them, and of kindred matters. All this is of
great help in understanding the mediaeval learning
packed into the *Commedia*. In these comments he
follows the accepted method of expounding first the
literal meaning and afterwards the allegorical mean-

ing. In the third treatise he explains that what, according to the bald meaning of the words, appears to be the passion of human love is really love of philosophy. In the fourth treatise he discourses at length upon the true nature of nobility. The other treatises, so far as we know, were never written.

Dante's learning was vast. He did not pursue learning for learning's sake nor out of intellectual curiosity, but because knowledge of all kinds, so he believed, is knowledge of God. The ultimate goal of all endeavor is to see God face to face, but in the meantime, before the soul is lifted up to such a height, the more the intellect understands of the workings of God's will in the universe, the nearer the soul comes to God. Two wings are necessary for the soul's flight, the heart and the intellect. To be sure one cannot know God unless one loves Him, but one cannot love Him as He deserves unless one knows Him. God is truth. Christ expressly said: "I am . . . the truth" (St. John xiv, 6). And truth, for men, is a knowledge of reality; and though it may be that the presence of God can be perceived more vividly in ecstatic vision, nevertheless in ordinary moments His presence can be perceived in all parts of creation. As a lover of art gets to know an artist by studying his works, so Dante believed that he attained, by amassing knowledge, to a clearer understanding of God.

St. Paul says: "God our Saviour . . . will have all men to be saved and to come into the knowledge of the truth" (I Tim. ii, 4). And Christ himself had said: "Ye shall know the truth and the truth shall

make you free" (St. John viii, 32). Truth is the
meeting of man's mind with God, and God —
though all these matters are beyond the plummet of
the human intellect — is present in all His works;
in them man still feels the pressure of His creative
hand, and touches the prints of His fingers. So —
Dante would say — by knowledge of matter and
energy, of time and space, of things metaphysical
and spiritual, the seeker after God enters into the
outer courts of His presence and feels the breathings
of His spirit. Not an ignorant and slothful intellect
can perceive God; but an intellect clarified and
stimulated by effort, an intellect that has sought
God everywhere, in all His handiwork, in the heavens
that declare His glory, in men, in beasts, in plants,
in all manifestations whatever of His power and
majesty. "Through knowledge shall the just be delivered" (Prov. xi, 9). So, Dante, with such hopes
and beliefs, in his exile and wanderings, in his poverty
and dependence upon others, steadily pressed on
upon the path of knowledge that his soul might at
last be permitted to see God face to face. And having
studied in order to help his own soul, he wrote *Il
Convivio* to help others, for as he says: "The principal
design of it is to lead men to knowledge and virtue"
(First treatise, ch. IX).

The *De Monarchia* is primarily a political treatise
on the relation between Church and State. It is
written in Latin, because Dante here is a scholar
talking to scholars. Taken together with the *Convivio* it shows how Dante's thought is gradually
moving towards the form it was finally to take in the

Commedia. The *Convivio* deals with one aspect of the problem that continually occupied him, how man shall pass from the confusion of sin to the ordered peace of the spirit; that aspect pointed to salvation through knowledge. The *De Monarchia* considers the same problem from a political, or social, point of view. Both, in their most serious meanings, make one prayer, "Grant us thy peace." If Dante had been a recluse, he would have concerned himself only with the soul and its spiritual salvation; but he was a man of action, full of compassion for mankind, and he would not be saved alone. For him the problems of salvation concerned social and political life as well as personal life. He felt with Tolstoi, — "They speak in vain who say that the Christian teaching touches the personal salvation, and not the general question of state" (*My Religion*, ch. III). Dante sought for the great law of spiritual gravitation that draws all things to God — "*quia fecisti nos ad te et inquietum est cor nostrum, donec requiescat in te,*" for Thou hast made us for Thyself, and our hearts are restless until they find rest in Thee (*St. Aug. Conf.* I, 1). The *De Monarchia* is an examination of the political basis necessary to enable that spiritual law to operate. Dante starts from the premise that the souls of men cannot attain to God unless they are free to busy themselves with the task of self-perfectioning; they must have full liberty for contemplation and for action. Such liberty cannot exist where there is social confusion; and social confusion will exist so long as there are a multitude of rulers, with selfish ambitions and interests, each covetous and grasping.

Tolstoi says the same thing: "The greatest welfare of man towards which all men aspire can only be obtained by perfect union and concord among men" (*Christian Teaching*). Tolstoi also says: "I not only know now that my separation from other nations is an evil which ruins my good: I know also the offense which has led me into this evil, and I can no longer, as I used to before, serve it calmly and consciously. I know that this offense consists in the delusion that my good is connected only with the good of my nation and not with the good of the whole world. Now I know that my union with other men cannot be impaired by a border line and by government decisions as to my belonging to this nation or to that. . . . I now understand the meaning of the words, Do good to your enemies; do to them what you would do to your own people. You are all the children of one Father; and be like your Father, that is make no division between your nation and another, — be alike to all. Now I understand that the good is possible for me only when I recognize the union with all men of the world without any exception."

Dante's theory was that the cure for divisions, hostility, and war between nation and nation, prince and prince, city and city, faction and faction, lies in bringing them all under one common government. To-day, still more poignantly, we feel the same need; and our remedy approximates to his, for we propose to bring all nations under the guidance of one supreme court in all matters of international dissension. By different roads we arrive at the same conclusion. There must be a monarch — a supreme will — that shall have power to settle quarrels, maintain peace, to decide between divergent national interests, and to spread good will among men. For us that monarch, that supreme will, must be composed of the coördinated wills of many nations; for Dante, it was the Emperor of the Holy Roman Empire, a ruler appointed by Divine Providence, and raised high above the temptations that beset lesser princes. We in America base our hopes in this respect on the analogy of the successful union of our forty-eight states united under one head; Dante based his hopes on the teaching of European history, that only the dominion of the Emperor of the Roman Empire could establish peace, order, justice, law.

The *De Monarchia* is divided into three parts. The first sets forth the need of monarchy for humanity; the second, the proofs that the Romans were God's chosen people, appointed by Him to establish universal monarchy; the third discusses the relations between this universal temporal rule of the Emperor and the universal spiritual rule of the papacy, and concludes that the right of the Roman Emperor is derived directly from God and is not dependent upon the papal will. From this the obvious inference is that the Pope must not cross the Emperor in temporal matters.

Under the government of an Emperor, raised above mortal temptations (so Dante thought), righteousness will flourish, men will find themselves equal to the task of combating evil, and able to give themselves to contemplation, to prayer, to a long-continued discipline of the senses, to things of the mind and things of the soul, and so, though the human heart will still need refining and purifying, they may have comfortable hope that in the end they shall attain to a knowledge and love of God.

In this way Dante, listening to the incantations of hope, lifted up his eyes above the battlements and castellated tops that shut in the narrow streets of Verona and Ravenna, above the towers of Bologna, beyond the clangor of warlike bells, and the vituperations of angry citizens, beyond the rough tops of the Apennines, beyond the steep stairs and the salt bread of exile, high above the grossness and cruelty of common life, and gazed at the starry sky, and believed that as God had established an order in heaven, so should an Emperor establish order on earth.

But after the death of Henry VII, his thoughts turned from outward peace to inward peace, and little by little he learned the supreme lesson of life, that the confusion which tosses us to and fro, and the peace that comforts and illumines us, are not in the material world without but in the spiritual world within, and pondering on this lesson, and having mastered the art of poetry, and having profoundly studied science and philosophy, he applied himself with all his heart and soul, and all his mind, to the great task to which he had dedicated himself in youth.

CHAPTER VII

THE INFERNO

THE *Commedia* consists of three parts, — the *Inferno*, the *Purgatorio*, and the *Paradiso*. Each part has thirty-three cantos, and the *Inferno* an introductory canto as well, so that in all there are a hundred. The verse is *terza rima*, a form virtually of Dante's own creating, the lines being grouped three by three, and each rime repeated thrice, in this fashion, A B A, B C B, C D C, and so on. At the beginning and end of each canto one of the three rimes is of necessity omitted. The line has eleven syllables as read aloud; but as a vowel at the end of a word is elided when the next word begins with a vowel, the reader often sees printed many more syllables than are pronounced.

Dante called the poem a *commedia*, because as with comedy it begins in a troublous and threatening situation and ends happily, and also because it is written in Italian, not Latin, and in a loose and simple manner (Letter to Can Grande, Sec. 10), in a less stately style than would befit tragedy (*De Vulg. El.* Book I, ch. IV). To this name posterity has prefixed the adjective *divine*. Boccaccio speaks of the *divina commedia*, but this phrase was not used as a title until an edition published in 1555.

The *Commedia* has two principal aspects, — literal and allegorical. Dante's contemporaries knew, without being told, and modern readers conversant with mediaeval literature know, that a poem written at the beginning of the fourteenth century on such a subject could not be a mere story, but must hold a deeper meaning in the allegory hidden beneath the letter. Nevertheless, Dante, having made the literal story as vivid and picturesque as language is able to do, is half afraid lest the attention of his readers may be absorbed by its fascination; therefore he reminds them again and again of the allegory underneath. In one of the early cantos of the *Inferno* he says:

> O voi, che avete gl' intelletti sani,
>   mirate la dottrina, che s'asconde
>   sotto il velame degli versi strani!

> O ye who have your understandings sound
>   Look at the teaching that lies hid
>   Under the veiling of these verses strange.

Inf. IX, 61–63

And he also did the same in the *Purgatorio:*

> Aguzza qui, lettor, ben gli occhi al vero,
>   chè il velo è ora ben tanto sottile,
>   certo, che il trapassar dentro è leggiero.

> Sharpen your eyes here, Reader, to the truth
>   Because the veil is now so very thin
>   That verily to pass within is easy.

Purg. VIII, 19–21

And a third time, in the dedicatory letter to Can Grande, which is a sort of preface to the *Paradiso*, he insists on the importance of the allegory. Dante

never forgot that he is a preacher, as well as a
prophet and poet.

In its literal aspect the *Inferno* is the hell of popular tradition, the abode of lost souls after death. It
is a great pit, shaped like a cone, growing narrower
and narrower, with its mouth under ground somewhere below Jerusalem, and its apex down at the
very center of the earth. In places this pit is encircled
by rugged ledges, and at others its sides are sheer
precipices of almost unimaginable depth. Round
these frightful circles, down these horrible abysses,
we accompany the poet. Every step of the way is as
vivid to our intelligence as objects of sight. Dante
begins by saying that in the mid-road of human life
he became aware that he was in a wild, dark wood,
and had lost his way; nevertheless he could see the
top of a sunlit mountain and was starting out
towards it when savage beasts rushed out and
frightened him so that he turned to go back. To
his great comfort he perceives some one coming. It
is the gracious Virgil, who tells him that to escape
from the wild wood he must take another way, and
that he will guide him through the darkness of Hell
and up through Purgatory. Dante shrinks back at
the mere thought of going down into Hell, but Virgil
inspires him with courage by recounting how Beatrice had come down from Heaven on purpose to
rescue him. So they set forth and pass through the
gate of Hell, under the terrible inscription, —

> lasciate ogni speranza, voi ch' entrate.

> All hope abandon ye who enter here.

> *Inf.* III, 9

There, in a sort of vestibule, Dante hears all the various sounds of woe. First are the cowards who evaded the responsibility of life, daring neither to do right nor to do wrong:

> Questo misero modo
> tengon l' anime triste di coloro,
> che visser senza infamia e senza lodo.
> Mischiate sono a quel cattivo coro
> degli angeli che non furon ribelli,
> nè fur fedeli a Dio, ma per sè foro.
> Cacciarli i ciel per non esser men belli,
> nè lo profondo inferno gli riceve,
> chè alcuna gloria i rei avrebber d' elli.

> This wretched kind of life
> the miserable spirits lead of those
> who lived with neither infamy nor praise.
> Commingled are they with that worthless choir
> of Angels who did not rebel, nor yet
> were true to God, but sided with themselves.
> The heavens, in order not to be less fair,
> expelled them; nor doth nether Hell receive them,
> because the bad would get some glory thence.

> *Inf*. III, 34–42, Langdon

Then the poets reach the river Acheron, across which Charon ferries them, and on the further side they come to Limbo, where they see the souls of those who never knew God, both the unbaptized and the heathen. After this they pass the great judge, Minos, and arrive at the circle where sins of the flesh are punished. Here they meet Francesca da Rimini, who tells her story, not outdone in tenderness even by the scene in *King Lear* where the poor old man slowly comes to his senses and recognizes his daughter

Cordelia (Act IV, scene VII). It is one of the perfect passages in all poetry. On the two poets go,
through the abode of gluttons, misers, prodigals, of
the wrathful, across the foul Stygian swamp, and
approach the city of Dis, the inner citadel of Hell.
Here a multitude of demons forbid their entrance, but
an angel descends from Heaven and drives them
back. They pass in, and see the punishment of here-
tics, among whom is Farinata degli Uberti; and,
further down, they walk round other circles peopled
by the souls of the violent, — tyrants, murderers,
conquerors, and suicides. Here is Pier della Vigna,
bosom counselor to Frederick II. Further down still
are those who have offended against the primal laws
of nature; among these is Brunetto Latini. Then
down into Malebolge (pouches of evil), where there
is a horrid succession of panders, seducers, flatterers,
simonists, magicians, cheats, hypocrites, thieves, and
evil counselors.

Here they meet Ulysses; and in meeting him, as in
meeting Pier della Vigna and Brunetto Latini, the
preacher and the prophet are lost in the poet, and
Dante, kindled to enthusiasm, gives rein to his
admiration. Ulysses tells the story of his last voyage,
how neither the sweet society of his son, nor filial
duty towards his old father, nor marital love for
Penelope, had been able to restrain his ardent curiosity to see the world; so he had put to sea with his
little band of comrades, and sailed westward through
the Mediterranean out past the pillars which Her-
cules had set as a mark that no man should venture
further:

"O frati", dissi, "che per cento milia
    perigli siete giunti all' occidente,
    a questa tanto picciola vigilia
de' vostri sensi, ch' è del rimanente,
    non vogliate negar l' esperienza,
    di retro al sol, del mondo senza gente.
Considerate la vostra semenza:
    fatti non foste a viver come bruti,
    ma per seguir virtute e conoscenza."

And then I said: "O brothers, ye who now
have through a hundred thousand perils reached
the West, to this so short a waking-time
still left your senses, will not to refuse
experience of that world behind the sun
which knows not man! Bethink you of the seed
whence ye have sprung; for ye were not created
to lead the life of stupid animals,
but manliness and knowledge to pursue."

                          Inf. XXVI, 112-120, LANGDON

After leaving Ulysses, Virgil and Dante take their
way still downward, towards the bottom of the pit,
where disloyalty shows its hideous character. Here
is the episode of Ugolino with his teeth in the skull
of Archbishop Ruggieri, both frozen in one hole
(*Inf.* XXXII–XXXIII). And at the very bottom of
the pit are the most horrid traitors of all, Cassius,
Brutus, Judas, and Satan himself, with no touch of
dignity or nobility, but foul, bestial, and loathsome.
This is the depth of Hell, the center of the earth; and
having descended to the central spot, the poets turn
and proceed upward by a little path that leads them
once more to the sweet air, at the antipodes of
Jerusalem, and they issue forth on the other side of

the world, "*a riveder le stelle*," "to see the stars
again," near the base of the Mount of Purgatory.

This is a wonderful narrative. The reader forgets
that he has not followed Virgil himself, so grimly all
the rugged path, the foul swamp, the great bowlders,
the fearful depths, the wretched men, and the mighty
servants of Hell have stood forth against the back-
ground of everlasting darkness. Never has a master
of words possessed so much of the power of the
painter, the sculptor, and the architect. Dante has
planned, digged, built, modeled, and colored. He
must have had a remarkable eye for visual effects.
Leonardi Bruni says: "*Di sua mano egregiamente
disegnava*," "with his own hand he drew extraordi-
narily well," and, in the *Vita Nuova*, Dante himself
speaks of drawing: "I betook myself to drawing the
likeness of an angel on my tablets"; but there needs
no evidence outside of the *Commedia* to show his
interest in all the arts; there one sees in the blossom
that Florentine delight in art of all kinds which
came to full flowering during the following centuries.

But to Dante this literal Hell was a secondary
matter; so it is to us. He and we are concerned with
the allegory. That allegory is simple. Hell is the
absence of God. Thomas à Kempis cried out: "Where
Thou art, there is heaven; and where Thou art not,
there is death and hell." Hell is the consequence of
sin, and sin is negation, a closing of the eyes to the
presence of God, a refusal to take His proffered
hand, a denial of all loyalty to the divine. Dante's
conception of sin is like that of all great moral
geniuses who have learned to know the peace and

joy of the presence of God. Sin is a turning away
from God. St. Augustine says: "I inquired what
iniquity might be, and I found it not to be a substance, but a swerving merely of the will, turned
quite away from Thee, O God . . . towards lowest
things" (*Conf.* VII, 16). But sin may be worse than
that. "Sin," John Bunyan said on his deathbed,
"turns all God's grace into wantonness; it is the
dare of His justice, the rape of His mercy, the jeer
of His patience, the slight of His power and the contempt of His love."

This is the awful thing, contempt of God's love.
It is God's love (manifested for most people in human
love) that constitutes goodness and happiness. If
men turn from love, they inflict upon themselves
their own punishment. God's presence, when intelligible to the human mind, is to be found in love, in
beauty, in radiance, in kindness, in joy, in work, in
sacrifice; and so to forsake Him, the Sum of Good,
is to descend into Hell. Dante's literal Hell is sin
made visible, palpable; his sinners are men living
in the dark pit of a consciousness wholly unillumined
by a knowledge or love of God. Pascal says: "Apart
from Jesus Christ is naught but vice and misery,
error and darkness, death and despair." Necessarily,
the soul that is in a state of sin does not behold the
manifestations of God; so in Dante's literal Hell there
are none of the signs and wonders of God that cheer
men upon earth, no warmth of the sun, no moonlight
on the waters, no birds singing, no noises of childhood, no dance of maidens, no nimbleness of youth,
no smiles, no laughs, no kindly human intercourse,

no flashes of heroism, no glamour of high romance, no thrill of self-sacrifice, no reachings of the mind toward infinite wisdom; but in their place envy, hatred, malice, bestiality, and fraud. The heart has become an unwatered desert where no good things grow.

This is the only explanation needed to understand the allegory, if this obvious explanation may be called necessary; all commentaries and notes serve only to confuse the reader whose object is spiritual light. This one key unlocks the whole inner meaning of all the episodes. If the reader begins with the consciousness that he is reading about sin, spiritually understood, he never loses the thread, he is never at a loss, never slips back into the literal signification. The meaning of the wild wood, of the beasts, is obvious. So Bunyan says, "Fears like masterless hell-hounds roared and bellowed in my soul." Virgil is unmistakably a wise guide who will lead a stray soul through the ways of sin and penitence, but cannot conduct it into the presence of God, because he himself does not know God. The gates of Hell, the murky Limbo, the circles, the precipices, the horrible coldness of the pit, need no interpreter. The *dramatis personae* of the hellish drama have received the stamp of individuality from the genius of the poet, and speak to Dante as man to man, but they are none the less types of sins such as the Apostle Paul speaks of: "Even as they did not like to retain God in their knowledge, God gave them over to a reprobate mind to do things which are not convenient; being filled with all unrighteousness, wickedness, covetousness, maliciousness, full of envy, murder, debate, deceit, malignity, whisperers, backbiters, haters of God, despiteful, proud, boasters, inventors of evil things, disobedient to parents, without understanding, covenant-breakers, without natural affection, implacable, unmerciful" (Rom. i, 28–31). "Their portion shall be indignation, wrath, tribulation and anguish" (Is. ii, 8–9). The ghosts of such sins, Dante saw in his descent into the lowest recesses of the human heart.

In *Pilgrim's Progress* the allegory is almost lost in the literal narrative, here the letter is almost lost in the allegory. For instance, the thirst of the forger Maestro Adamo is an obvious allegory of the thirst for innocence:

> Lasso! un gocciol d' acqua bramo.
> Li ruscelletti, che dei verdi colli
>   del Casentin discendon giuso in Arno,
>   facendo i lor canali freddi e molli,
> sempre mi stanno innanzi.

> Alas! I crave a drop of water.
> The little brooks which toward the Arno run
> down from the Casentino's green-clad hills,
> and render all their channels cool and fresh
> are evermore before me.
>
> *Inf.* XXX, 63–67, LANGDON

Likewise what fitter description of a glutton's spiritual atmosphere can there be than in these lines?

> Grandine grossa, e acqua tinta, e neve
>   per l'aer tenebroso si riversa;
>   pute la terra che questo riceve.

Coarse hail, and snow and dirty-colored water
through the dark air are ever pouring down;
and foully smells the ground receiving them.

Inf. VI, 10–12, LANGDON

And what can depict the mad fury of rage better
than this?

Qual è quel toro che si slaccia in quella
  che ha ricevuto già 'l colpo mortale,
  che gir non sa, ma qua e là saltella;
vid' io lo Minotauro far cotale;

As doth a bull, who from his leash breaks free
the moment he receives the mortal blow,
and cannot walk but plunges here and there;
so doing I beheld the Minotaur.

Inf. XII, 22–25, LANGDON

CHAPTER VIII

OTHER ASPECTS OF THE INFERNO

EVERYWHERE the allegory constitutes the great body of the poem, in all its parts and members, while the literal story is a mere skin or covering. And yet under the allegory lies a personal confession. It is impossible to read the *Inferno* and not know that the poet who wrote it had committed sin. The only mistake might be to think his sin more heinous than it was. No doubt every sensitive spiritual soul who has done wrong and repented, when he looks back upon his wrongdoing inclines to magnify its wickedness. St. Augustine distorted robbing his neighbor's pear tree into a sin; and Bunyan suffered because he had played hit-the-stick on Sunday. But allowing for exaggeration, it is true, as Bunyan said, "How can he tell what it is to be saved, that hath not in his own conscience groaned under the burden of sin?" Spiritual souls may be morbid and convert trivial misdoing into wickedness, but that is because they understand what it is to be cut off from the knowledge and love of God; whereas ordinary men, with what they call a healthy tendency to make the best of things, incline to look upon their sins as trivial and excusable.

Some of Dante's wrongdoing we learned in another

chapter. The sin of incontinence, however gross it appeared to him in the presence of Beatrice, he recognized to be the sin most readily pardoned. In Hell it receives the lightest punishment. That is because this sin is sometimes ennobled by love, as with Paolo and Francesca; and yet in spite of its romantic glamour, Dante saw the ugliness of the sin which disfigures the beauty of love. St. Augustine looked back on his backslidings in the same manner: "And what was it that I delighted in, but to love and be loved? but out of the puddly concupiscence of my flesh, certain mists and bubblings of youth fumed up, which beclouded and so overcast my heart, that I could not discern the beauty of a chaste affection from a fog of impure lustfulness. Both did confusedly boil in me, and ravished away my unstayed youth over the downfalls of unchaste desires, and drenched me over head and ears in the very whirlpool of most heinous impurities" (*Conf.* II, 2, translation by WATTS). But Dante was aware of a deeper and subtler sin, the sin of pride. Of this sin, Satan, "king over all the children of pride" (Job xli, 34), is the great symbol. In the days before the war, old traditional notions of chivalry, of gentility, of what were called birth and honor, prevented most men from understanding the true nature of pride; the phrase "proper pride" was judged an acceptable excuse for many an act of unchristian conduct. The Church had accomplished little or nothing by classifying pride as one of the seven deadly sins. But now that we see how pride of dynasty, pride of caste, pride of race, pride of accomplishment, pride of power, have wrought a

world of woe, we understand better the nature of
pride, that it is indeed a deadly sin.

Coleridge says of it: "In its utmost abstraction
and consequent state of reprobation, the Will becomes satanic pride and rebellious self-idolatry in
the relations of the spirit to itself, and remorseless
despotism relatively to others; the more hopeless
as the more obdurate by its subjugation of sensual
impulses, by its superiority to toil and pain and
pleasure: in short, by the fearful resolve to find in
itself alone the one absolute motive of action, under
which all other motives from within and from without
must be either subordinated or crushed. . . . Wherever it has appeared, under whatever circumstances
of time and country . . . it has been identified by
the same attributes. Hope, in which there is no
cheerfulness; steadfastness within and immovable
resolve, with outward restlessness and whirling
activity; violence with guile; temerity with cunning;
and, as the result of all, interminableness of object
with perfect indifference of means" (*Lay Sermons*,
quoted in *The Spirit of Man*, No. 274). Dante was
a proud man, but with his clear spiritual insight he
recognized the wickedness of pride and the virtue of
humility.

Giovanni Villani says: "*Questo Dante per lo suo
sapere fu alquanto presontuoso e schifo e isdegnoso*,"
— "This Dante on account of his learning was
somewhat arrogant, fastidious, and disdainful"; and
Boccaccio, "*Fu il nostro Poeta, . . . di animo alto
e disdegnoso molto*," — "Our poet was of a high spirit
and very disdainful." Boccaccio also tells a story,

foolish in itself, which serves to show Dante's popular reputation. A proposal was made for the government of Florence to send an embassy to Pope Boniface, and it was suggested that Dante should be at the head of it; whereupon he said: "*Se io vo, chi rimane? se io rimango, chi va?*" "If I go, who stays? If I stay, who goes?" That is mere gossip; but his pride is well shown in his letter refusing to accept the pardon proffered to exiles by the Florentine government; it also betrays itself in many places in the *Commedia*. The wickedness of pride is that it substitutes self-will in place of the will of God; like leaven, it puffs up every sin, and pushed to extreme becomes rank disloyalty to God, as in Lucifer. It mocks the prayer that Jesus taught to all men, "Thy will be done." Dante knew his own weakness, and knew it to be sin, the cause of sorrow and suffering.

But Dante is not thinking only of himself; he is a prophet yearning over people who like silly sheep follow a false show of pleasure and turn their backs on God. So, in the *Inferno*, he does not confine himself to his own sins, but enumerates all the categories, so that we all may find our own wrongdoings bodied forth, whether they are due to incontinence, to anger and violence, or to disloyalty towards what we feel is the highest. Dante is possessed by the thought that no man leads his life alone, that we are all members of the great body corporate of humanity, bound together for better, for worse; therefore, in his narrative of his own descent into Hell, he is also the representative of humanity. His experience is the experience of the race. Dante is full of this feel-

ing of his identity with mankind. For instance, during
humanity's pilgrimage through the dark places of
mortal life, Christ had come into the world and
shewed men the true light (St. John i, 9); in like
manner, Beatrice, who is also an emanation from
God, had shown the true light to him (*V. N.* XXIV).
So all through the poem we find meaning intertwined
with meaning, allegory blended with allegory.

However much we may be absorbed in the inner
meanings of the poem, we cannot escape from admiration for the amazing skill with which the poet has
kept letter and allegory so intricately united, and
so distinct and separate. The two are like brain and
mind, seeming to keep arm-in-arm forever, and yet
with nothing in common, the one tangible, visible,
material, the other an unknown, magic essence.
Dante is a master craftsman, and, when he will, a
master artist. Homer, it is said, nods, and Shakespeare, it is certain, writes loose bombast; but Dante
is always alert and concentrated on his task, always
lord of his material. It is so from the first line of the
first canto, and so it continues.

To appreciate his poetry, his art, and his power of
combining allegory and story, one need but read the
beautiful passage in the second canto, in which
Dante, by drawing down to the confines of Hell the
glorious light of Paradise, emphasizes the blackness
of the abode of sinners. Virgil tells Dante how
Beatrice sent him to rescue him:

> Io era tra color, che son sospesi,
> e donna mi chiamò beata e bella,
> tal, che di comandare io la richiesi.

Lucevan gli occhi suoi più che la stella;
  e cominciommi a dir soave e piana,
  con angelica voce, in sua favella:
" O anima cortese Mantovana,
  di cui la fama ancor nel mondo dura,
  e durerà quanto il moto lontana!
l'amico mio, e non della ventura,
  nella diserta piaggia è impedito
  sì nel cammin, che volto è per paura;
temo che non sia già sì smarrito,
  ch'io mi sia tardi al soccorso levata,
  per quel ch'io ho di lui nel Cielo udito.
Or muovi, e con la tua parola ornata,
  e con ciò, ch' è mestieri al suo campare,
  l'aiuta sì, ch'io ne sia consolata.
Io son Beatrice, che ti faccio andare;
  vegno di loco, ove tornar disio,
  amor mi mosse, che mi fa parlare.

.   .   .   .

Donna è gentil nel Ciel, che si compiange
  di questo impedimento, ov' io ti mando,
  sì che duro giudizio lassù frange.
Questa chiese Lucia in suo dimando,
  e disse: 'Or ha bisogno il tuo fedele
  di te, ed io a te lo raccomando.'
Lucia, nimica di ciascun crudele,
  si mosse, e venne al loco dov' io era,
  che mi sedea con l'antica Rachele.
Disse: 'Beatrice, loda di Dio vera
  che non soccorri quei che t'amò tanto,
  che uscìo per te della volgare schiera?
Non odi tu la pieta del suo pianto?
  Non vedi tu la morte che il combatte
  su la fiumana, ove il mar non ha vanto?'

Al mondo non fur mai persone ratte
  a far lor pro, nè a fuggir lor danno,
  com'io, dopo cotai parole fatte,

venni quaggiù dal mio beato scanno,
  fidandomi del tuo parlare onesto,
  che onora te, e quei che udito l'hanno."
Poscia che m'ebbe ragionato questo,
  gli occhi lucenti lagrimando volse;
  per che mi fece del venir più presto;
e venni a te così, com' ella volse;
  dinanzi a quella fiera ti levai,
  che del bel monte il corto andar ti tolse.

Among the intermediate souls I was,
when me a Lady called, so beautiful
and happy, that I begged her to command.
Her eyes were shining brighter than a star,
when sweetly and softly she began to say,
as with an angel's voice she spoke to me:
" O courteous Mantuan spirit, thou whose fame
is still enduring in the world above,
and will endure as long as lasts the world,
a friend of mine, but not a friend of Fortune,
is on his journey o'er the lonely slope
obstructed so, that he hath turned through fear;
and, from what I have heard of him in Heaven,
I fear lest he may now have strayed so far,
that I have risen too late to give him help.
Bestir thee, then, and with thy finished speech,
and with whatever his escape may need,
assist him so that I may be consoled.
I, who now have thee go, am Beatrice;
thence come I, whither I would fain return;
t'was love that moved me, love that makes me speak.

. . . .

There is a Gentle Lady up in Heaven,
who grieves so at this check, whereto I send thee,
that broken is stern judgment there above.
She called Lucia in her prayer, and said:
' Now hath thy faithful servant need of thee,
and I, too, recommend him to thy care.'
Lucia, hostile to all cruelty,

set forth thereat, and came unto the place,
where I with ancient Rachel had my seat.
'Why, Beatrice,' she said, 'true Praise of God,
dost thou not succour him who loved thee so,
that for thy sake he left the common herd?
Dost thou not hear the anguish of his cry?
See'st not the death that fights him on the flood,
o'er which the sea availeth not to boast?'
Ne'er were there any in the world so swift
to seek their profit and avoid their loss,
as I, after such words as these were uttered,
descended hither from my blesséd seat,
confiding in that noble speech of thine,
which honors thee and whosoe'er has heard it."
Then, after she had spoken to me thus,
weeping she turned her shining eyes away;
which made me hasten all the more to come;
and, even as she wished, I came to thee,
and led thee from the presence of the beast,
which robbed thee of the fair Mount's short approach.

Inf. II, 52–72, 94–120, Langdon

On the surface Dante is often subtle, scholastic, hairsplitting, so that the shell of the *Commedia* becomes crabbed and hieroglyphic; and that is why there are so many commentaries; but every now and then, underneath this mediaeval casing, his passion for righteousness and his poetic soul rise up in their strength, bursting through obsolete science, outworn theology, and forgotten history, as Samson burst free from the bondage of green withes, and embody themselves in immortal verse.

CHAPTER IX

THE PURGATORIO

GEORGE FOX, the founder of the Quakers, in his journal says: "I saw that there was an ocean of darkness and death; but an infinite ocean of light and love, which flowed over the ocean of darkness." This is also Dante's experience, light above darkness, and the experience of almost every man who seeks for spiritual life, however different the words may be in which different men clothe their experiences. Dante had seen spiritual darkness and spiritual death, and now he perceived the radiance of spiritual light and spiritual love.

The literal Mount of Purgatory is on an island on the side of the earth opposite Jerusalem; this island is encircled by the sea upon which the adventurous Ulysses and his mariners were drowned. The shore and the lower slopes of the mountain are but approaches, or ante-Purgatory, for Purgatory itself is the main ascent. Round and round the mountain, mounting by steep stairs from ledge to ledge, the rugged path slowly climbs. On different ledges, different sins are expiated in the order of their gravity, — pride, envy, anger, sloth, avarice, gluttony, and sensuality. At last, having reached the top, the pilgrim, purified and washed clean, even of the memory of his sins, in the river Lethe, enters into the Earthly Paradise, the home of innocence.

Seekers after the spiritual life want to know from Dante's experience how they, too, can pass from sin into the state of blessedness, how they shall learn to mount upwards, who or what will be their helpers, and whence shall come their strength. Therefore, the allegory rather than the literal narrative is our immediate concern, so let us follow the allegory.

At the opening of the first canto the poet says:

> E canterò di quel secondo regno,
>   dove l'umano spirito si purga
>   e di salire al ciel diventa degno,

> And I will sing of that second kingdom
>   Where the human soul is purified
>   And becomes worthy to mount to Heaven.
>
> *Purg.* I, 4–6

The essence of Hell is the darkness that is caused by the complete absence of God; whereas in Purgatory the light of God shines roundabout. No sooner has Dante emerged from the darkness of sin than his soul is bathed by this light;

> Dolce color d'oriental zaffiro
>   che s' accoglieva nel sereno aspetto
>   dell' aer puro . . .
> agli occhi miei ricominciò diletto,
>   tosto ch' i' uscii fuor dell' aura morta.

> Sweet color of orient sapphire
>   That was deepening in the serene aspect
>   Of the stainless air . . .
> To my eyes brought back delight,
>   As soon as I had issued forth from the dead air.
>
> *Ib.* 13–17

This is the radiance of joy on abandoning sin. So
St. Augustine, emerging from the follies of his youth,
says: "Into my heart I entered and with the eyes of
my soul I saw above . . . the unchangeable Light. . . .
He that knoweth Truth, knoweth that light, and
he that knoweth that light, knoweth eternity"
(Conf. Book VII, ch. X).

Light is the great gift of God to those that turn
towards Him; that light illumines the penitents on
their way up the mountain, and when it is not shining they cannot see to go;

> andar su di notte non si puote,
>
> There is no going up by night.
>
> *Purg.* VII, 44

Besides light, which gives color and joy to all things
on the purifying way, there is another ripening and
mellowing influence, the hope of peace; and, as on
earth the wishing of peace — *Pax tibi, Pax huic
domo* — was the familiar salutation enjoined by
Christ to His apostles, so now to the repentant spirit
on its upward way this hope comes like a divine
greeting from Christ Himself. To Dante there was
music in the word; and no other that he uses is so
charged with pathos. In the *Inferno*, Francesca da
Rimini, whirled along forever by the infernal blast,
stirs our compassion to its depths by her unconscious
envy of the river that can find peace at last:

> Siede la terra, dove nata fui,
>   su la marina dove il Po discende
>   per aver pace

The town where I was born sits on the shore,
Whither the Po descends to be at peace.

Inf. V, 97–99

It is the episode of Dante's longing for peace that
gives verisimilitude to the Fra Ilario letter. And in the
De Monarchia, Dante says: "*Patet quod genus hu-
manum in quiete sive tranquillitate pacis ad proprium
suum opus, quod fere divinum est (juxta illud: Mi-
nuisti eum paulo minus ab angelis), liberrime atque
facillime se habet. Unde manifestum est, quod pax
universalis est optimum eorum, quod ad nostram
beatitudinem ordinantur. Hinc est, quod pastoribus de
sursum sonuit, non divitiae, non voluptates, non ho-
nores, non longitudo vitae, non sanitas, non robur, non
pulchritudo; sed pax. Inquit enim coelestis militia:
'Gloria in altissimis Deo, et in terra pax hominibus
bonae voluntatis.' Hinc etiam 'Pax vobis,' Salus
hominum salutabat. Decebat enim summum Salva-
torem, summam salutationem exprimere.*" — "It is evi-
dent that in the quiet or tranquillity of peace the
human race is most freely and favorably disposed
towards the work proper to it (which is almost
divine, even as it is said 'Thou hast made him a
little lower than the angels'). Whence it is manifest
that universal peace is the best of all those things
which are ordained for our blessedness. And that is
why there rang out to the shepherds from on high,
not riches, not pleasures, not honours, not length of
life, not health, not strength, not beauty, but peace.
For the celestial soldiery proclaims, 'Glory to God
in the highest; and, on earth, peace to men of good

will.' Hence also, 'Peace be with you' was the salutation of him who was the salvation of man. For it was meet that the supreme saviour should utter the supreme salutation" (First Book, Ch. IV, Temple Classics).

In Purgatory this hope of peace is a presentiment of Paradise, as sweet odors from shore are wafted out over the tumultuous ocean. In Paradise the soul is at one with God and therefore there is perfect peace; nevertheless, wherever God's will is done, even in the pains of Purgatory, there is peace, though not the perfect peace that comes when His will is done perfectly. And, while Francesca's allusion to peace in the *Inferno* is full of despair, the references in the *Purgatorio* are all full of hope. For instance, before the two poets find the entrance to Purgatory, and are wandering about the region below, Virgil asks the way of spirits whom he sees,

> per quella pace
> ch'io credo che per voi tutti si aspetti,

> by that peace
> which I believe you all await,
>
> *Purg.* III, 74–75

And Dante utters the word as the strongest asseveration:

> io farò per quella pace,
> che, retro ai piedi di sì fatta guida,
> di mondo in mondo cercar mi si face.

> I will for that peace' sake
> Which, close upon the steps of such a guide,
> From world to world draws me to follow it.
>
> *Purg.* V, 61–63

So, too, when the poet Statius meets them, his greeting is:

> Frati miei, Dio vi dea pace,

> My brothers, God give you peace,
>> *Purg.* XXI, 13

And Virgil returns the wish; and to another company of spirits, Dante says:

> O anime sicure
> d' aver, quando che sia, di pace stato,

> O souls, sure to obtain,
> Whenever it may be, the state of peace.
>> *Purg.* XXVI, 54

Virgil, also, in speaking of the lessons of Purgatory calls them

> acque della pace
> che dall' eterno fonte son diffuse,

> Waters of peace
> That from the Eternal Fount are poured forth.
>> *Purg.* XV, 131–132

And the prayer, "O Lamb of God, who takest away the sins of the world, grant us Thy peace" is uttered by the spirits who expiate the sin of wrath (*Purg.* XVI, 19).

To take away sin and to bestow peace are one and the same thing; it is for this that Purgatory is established. And, therefore, when having passed through Purgatory, the two pilgrims reach the Terrestrial Paradise, Virgil says to Dante:

Quel dolce pome, che per tanti rami
cercando va la cura dei mortali,
oggi porrà in pace le tue fami.

That sweet fruit, for which on many boughs
mankind goes seeking anxiously,
today will grant thy hunger peace.

Purg. XXVII, 115–117

The fruit Virgil speaks of is the peace of God, which
will come, as the Psalmist says, to the man purified
from all guile: "Mark the perfect man, and behold
the upright, for the end of that man is peace"
(Psalm xxxvii, 37).

On its journey up the mountain, lighted by the
divine light and cheered by the prospect of the peace
of God, the soul is purified. The method of purification is set out in detail, for Dante is a practical
preacher. First the pilgrim must start upon his way
with Fortitude, Temperance, Prudence and Justice,
shining like a constellation above him (*Purg.* I, 23),
he must also wash off the stains of sin (*Ib.* 128–129);
but these are minor matters: the four great helps
to climb the mountain are four sorts of spiritual
discipline — effort, prayer, divine grace, and pain.
Purgatory is a steep ascent; the road is hard and
dolorous. To the ordinary man effort is the help
nearest at hand. By putting forth his strength he
draws himself back from temptation, from the
appetites of the flesh, from the vanities of the world,
from hardness of heart, from all ignoble satisfaction
in unworthy things. He practices self-denial, he
ordains self-discipline; and, little by little, setting

his teeth and clenching his fists, by daily taking heed, by contrivances and devices to outwit his old self, he fashions new habits, and bursts at last the bonds of his servitude and enters into the perfect freedom of the service of God; — *libertà va cercando,* he goes in quest of freedom (*Purg.* I, 71), as Dante puts it.

The effort necessary to climb, Dante indicates by describing how steep the path is:

> Noi divenimmo intanto al piè del monte:
> quivi trovammo la roccia sì erta,
> che indarno vi sarien le gambe pronte.
> Tra Lerici e Turbia, la più diserta,
> la più romita via è una scala,
> verso di quella, agevole ed aperta.

> Meantime we came unto the mountain's foot:
> And here we found the crag so sheer
> That agile legs would not avail a man.
> Compared with this the wildest, loneliest way,
> From Lerici to Turbia, is like a stair
> Ample and easy.
>
> *Purg.* III, 46–51

> Vassi in Sanleo, e discendesi in Noli;
> montasi su Bismantova in cacume
> con esso in piè: ma qui convien ch' uom voli;
> dico con l'ali snelle e con le piume
> del gran disio.

> A man can walk at Sanleo and go down at Noli,
> He can climb to the very top of Bismantova,
> Upon his feet; but here a man must fly;
> I mean with the swift wings and pinions
> Of a great desire.
>
> *Purg.* IV, 25–29

But the more the efforts are repeated the easier they become.

> Questa montagna è tale,
> che sempre al cominciar di sotto è grave,
> E quanto uom più va su, e men fa male.

> Such is this mountain,
> That always the beginning down below
> Is hard, but the toil lessens as you rise.

Purg. IV, 88–90

The second help is prayer. Prayer is almost an instinctive reaction from a consciousness of sin. St. John of the Cross says: "Broken with grief, stricken by a fear that penetrates to the bottom of the heart at sight of the danger she is in of being lost, the soul renounces all worldly things; she forsakes all else, and delaying not for a day, not for an hour, with a heart full of groanings, already wounded by the divine love, she begins to call upon her Beloved" (*Canticle of the Spirit*, Sec. 1). The experience of humanity testifies that the mind, by fixing its gaze upon some selected symbol of the highest good, whether in silent contemplation or with spoken words, is steadied and acquires a poise, and from this steadiness and poise gains strength, so that it is enabled to slough off old habits and put on new, and shift the center round which revolves its world of hopes and fears. The range of prayer is very great, from the formal movements of the logical mind, through invocation, confession, and petition, or from the impetuous cry of the hungry heart for something vast and abiding, all the way to silent adoration, or to the mental endeavor, by subtle psychical practices, to open the windows of the soul upon some starry sky. Draw it out into a litany or compress it to a cry, the yearning is the same: *Angusta est domus animae meae, quo venias ad eam; dilatetur abs te. Ruinosa est; refice eam. Habet quae offendant oculos tuos, fateor et scio. Sed quis mundabit eam? Aut cui alteri praeter te clamabo? Ab occultis meis munda me, Domine, et ab alienis parce servo tuo.* — Narrow is the house of my soul for Thee to enter in; make Thou it wide. It lies in ruins; build Thou it up. I confess, I know, that there is that within it which will offend Thine eyes, But who shall cleanse it? Or, to whom but Thee shall I cry? Cleanse Thou me from secret sin, O Lord, and keep back Thy servant from presumptuous faults" (*St. Aug. Conf.* Book I, Ch. 5).

The necessity of prayer Dante reiterates. In the precincts outside of Purgatory an angel approaches, and Virgil cries out:

> Fa, fa che le ginocchia cali;
> ecco l'Angel di Dio: piega le mani:

> Bend, bend thy knees;
> Behold the angel of God, fold thy hands.
> *Purg.* II, 28–29

At the gate of Purgatory they find another angel sitting. Virgil again bids Dante pray:

> " Chiedi
> umilemente che il serrame scioglia."
> Divoto mi gittai a' santi piedi;
> misericordia chiesi che m'aprisse.

"Beg
Humbly that he undo the lock."
Devoutly I threw myself at his holy feet;
And begged, for mercy's sake, that he would
open to me.

Purg. IX, 108–110

On the lowest ledge of Purgatory, the proud in aid
of penitence repeat the Lord's prayer (*Purg.* XI,
1–21); other spirits pray that the living may not
omit praying for them (*Purg.* VI, 26). And elsewhere
a litany (XIII, 50–51), psalms (XXIII, 11), hymns
(XXV, 121), and the beatitudes (XII, 110, XV, 38,
etc.) are sung. And, with transparent allegory, Virgil
prays to the sun:

O dolce lume, a cui fidanza i' entro
per lo nuovo cammin, tu ne conduci.

O sweet light, through trust in which I enter
In this unknown way, lead thou us on.

Purg. XIII, 16–17

Prayer is the conscious yearning of the soul; but
deeper than prayer, more accomplishing than personal effort, are the workings of what theologians
call the grace of God. Down in that deep, mysterious
self, whose beginning and end we do not know,
strange processes take place; and, now and again,
as if a loadstone heaved its top above the surface
of that dim, vast unconsciousness, and swung the
needle of our compass north to south, some force
shoots up and readjusts all our life. "In the hidden
part Thou shalt make me to know wisdom" (Psalm
li, 6). There conversions take place; there Paul was
caught up to the third heaven; there Luther underwent his illumination that "The just shall live by

faith"; there St. Augustine heard the voice say
"*Tolle, lege*"; there Socrates was visited by his
familiar spirit; there Pascal had his revelation of fire;
there St. Francis received the stigmata; and there
many others, less famous, have been "touched by
the hand of God." Down in these depths (it seems)
a word, a touch, a look, lies like a germinating seed,
swells and grows, then blossoms and bears, until at
last our waking consciousness that ministers to
daily needs, inwardly roused, stretches forth its
hand, plucks the fruit, and finds that it holds the
fruit of the tree of life. Call them subliminal, transcendental, real, mystic, neurasthenic, hysterical, or
what you will, these processes take place in modes
still dark to human understanding. All that is certain
is that a change takes place. The animal instinct
of self-preservation and its fellow impulses no longer
control the soul's destiny, but new forces, inaudible,
invisible, intangible, lead it on a mysterious path,
while outsiders look on and marvel; as when deaf
old people seeing children in a room begin dancing
to music played in the street, hearing nothing,
think them wayward and fantastic.

When the soul feels this great shift of the center
of spiritual gravity, it explains the shock as best it
may. Formerly the terms of explanation were chiefly
theological, now they are taken from psychology.
George Fox says: "When all my hopes in [priests
and preachers] and in all men were gone, so that
I had nothing outwardly to help me, nor could I tell
what to do, then, oh then, I heard a voice which
said, 'There is one, even Christ Jesus, that can speak

to thy condition'; and when I heard it my heart did leap for joy" (*Journal*, Ch. I). And in the biography of St. Francis of Assisi it is written: "Being led by the spirit St. Francis went in [to the Church of S. Damiano] to pray; and he fell down before the crucifix in devout supplication, and having been smitten by unwonted visitations, found himself *another man* than he who had gone in" (quoted in *Mysticism*, E. Underhill, p. 218). And St. Catherine of Siena, after a vision in which Christ seemed to take her heart from her breast and put His there in its stead, said to her confessor: "Do you not see, Father, that I am no longer the person I was, but that I am changed into some one else? . . . Oh, Father, I firmly believe that if any one should feel the things that I feel within, no one is so hard-hearted, but he would become softened, none so proud but he would become humble. . . . My mind is in such a state of joy and jubilee that I am amazed how my soul can stay in my body. . . . This ardor produces in my mind a renewal of innocence and humility, as if I had gone back to be four or five years old. Besides it has kindled such love of my neighbor, that for any neighbor I would voluntarily and with great pleasure in my heart and joy in my mind, give up my mortal life" (*Vita*, Part II, Ch. VI, Sec. 4).

Madame Guyon, one of the famous mystics, tells how she had been seeking the presence of God in vain, and how her confessor had said to her: "Madam, you are seeking without, that which you have within. Accustom yourself to seek God in your own heart, and you will find him"; these words, she says, "were as an arrow, which pierced my soul through and through. I felt in this moment a profound wound, which was full of delight and of love —a wound so sweet that I desired it might never heal" (quoted in *Mysticism*, E. Underhill, pp. 222–223). And Brother Lawrence said that his conversion took place in this manner: "That in the winter, seeing a tree stripped of its leaves, and considering that within a little time the leaves would be renewed, and after that the flowers and fruit appear, he received a high view of the providence and power of God, which has never been effaced from his soul, and that this view had perfectly set him loose from the world" (*Brother Lawrence*, First Conversation).

These witnesses, and a multitude of others, confirm what Emerson says: "There is a difference between one and another hour of life, in their authority and subsequent effect. Our faith comes in moments. . . . Yet there is a depth in those brief moments which constrains us to ascribe more reality to them than to all other experiences" (*The Over-soul*).

It may be that human nature is of itself pure and holy, and that, when the animal personality is shaken off, it loses its warped and corrupt shapelessness and reassumes its natural beauty; or, it may be that there is a spiritual order that lies over our carnal order, as life lies over the inorganic world, and that these mysterious forces are "high instincts" from that upper region; or, it may be, as the Apostle puts it, that "God's love is shed abroad in our hearts by the Holy Ghost" (Rom. v, 5).

Tolstoi, the greatest religious teacher of our time, says: "What takes place is similar to what happens in the material world at every birth. The fruit is not born because it wants to be born, because it is better for it to be born, and because it knows that it is good to be born, but because it is nature, and it cannot continue its former existence; it is compelled to surrender to the new life, not so much because the new life calls it, as because the possibility of the former existence is destroyed. . . . What takes place is precisely what happens at the inception of everything: the same destruction of the seed, of the previous form of life, and the appearance of a new growth; the same seeming struggle of the older form of the decomposing seed and the increase of the new growth, and the same nutrition of the new growth at the expense of the decomposing seed. . . . We cannot see the birth of the new essence, the new relation of the rational consciousness [this is his term for the new directing power] to the animal, just as the seed cannot see the growth of its stalk. When the rational consciousness comes out of its concealed position and is made manifest for us, it seems to us that we are experiencing a contradiction. But there is no contradiction, just as there is none in the sprouting seed. In the sprouting seed, we see only that life, which before was in the integument of the seed, is now in its sprout. Even so there is no contradiction in man with his awakened rational consciousness, but only the birth of a new being, of a new relation of the rational consciousness to the animal" (*On Life*, Ch. IX.)

The coming of this new life is but another name
for the operation of grace. For Dante the divine
grace is always at work. It was of divine grace that
the Virgin Mary bestirred Lucia to send Beatrice
to Dante's rescue, when he was lost in the wild
wood. The commentators delight in theological
niceties, and therefore give several names — divine
mercy, illuminating grace, theology — to divine grace
as it flows down from its source, like geographers
who give different names to a river, in its upper
reaches, in its main channel, and at its mouth;
but, in truth, grace is the going forth of power from
the deeps of life, directly or indirectly, to the in-
dividual soul that needs it.

In the *Purgatorio* the operation of grace is plainly
visible. At the very beginning of Dante's journey in
ante-Purgatory, Cato, the warder, stops them, until
Virgil tells him that Beatrice has bidden them make
the journey:

> Dell' alto scende virtù che m'aiuta,

> From on high comes down the power that aids me.
> *Purg.* I, 68

And when Dante has only gone part way to Purgatory proper, with still a steep stretch to go, he lies
down and sleeps, and on waking finds that he has
been carried up to the very entrance of Purgatory.
Virgil explains how:

> Dianzi, nell' alba che precede al giorno,
>   quando l' anima tua dentro dormia
>   sopra li fiori, onde laggiù è adorno,
> venne una donna, e disse: " Io son Lucia;

lasciatemi pigliar costui che dorme,
sì l'agevolerò per la sua via "

.   .   .   .

ella ti tolse, e come il dì fu chiaro
sen venne suso, ed io per le sue orme.
Qui ti posò.

But now, just at the dawning that precedes the day,
    When thy soul lay asleep upon the flowers
    With which the place down there is beautified,
A Lady came and said, " I am Lucia,
    Let me pick up this sleeper here
    And I will help him nimbly on his way."

.   .   .   .

She took thee up, and when the day was bright
    Came up and laid thee here, while I
Went following in her steps.

Purg. IX, 52–61

And after Dante has fallen on his knees and said a
prayer, the angel guarding the gate of Purgatory
unlocks it for him to enter. Indeed, in one sense, the
whole ascent is a consequence of the action of grace,
although the poet does not essay to determine where
effort and prayer end and where grace begins.

Howbeit, whether the pilgrim climbs the Mount of
Purgatory by means of effort, prayer, or grace, he
cannot escape the law of purification through pain.
However incomprehensible that law is, it is but of a
piece with all the mystery of life. We are aware
of phenomena of all kinds that uprise above the
horizon of our consciousness and, after a brief day,
go to their setting, but of the whence, whither, wherefore, we know nothing. We can but strive to discern
the pattern in the stuff of life as it passes, and in that

pattern is the never ending embroidery of pain. If life has a meaning, pain shares in it; if life has a purpose, pain furthers it. If, as Dante believed, there is a kingdom of God within us, its foundation can only stand secure where sin has been dug up; and its mansions must be constructed out of the consciousness, whether illusory or not, of a divine presence, and pain is the master builder. This Dante felt. The pains which the penitents undergo on the different ledges of Purgatory are not punishments, much less revenge; they are the consciousness of sin. The haughty, who with swollen self-complacency had carried their load of pride, now that they are inspired with a desire to mount upward to the Highest, feel crushed down by their intolerable burden (*Purg.* Cantos X and XI). The envious, who chafed in displeasure at the joy of others, now realize the reason that they did not see the beauty of others' happiness was because their own eyelids, like those of young falcons in training time, were sewn together, and they weep for the ignominy of such blindness (Cantos XIII and XIV). Men of wrath now perceive that they were shut out from all delight by the black choking fog of their own evil passions, and they pray to be set free. And so in the other ledges. Nevertheless, it is hard for human nature to give up its passions, its vices, its love of ease; and the gradual weaning of the soul, prompted by the love of God, is fraught with pain. Death to sin is dying in a familiar part of oneself, and brings a mortal pang. But at last when the love of God triumphs, and the soul casts off her sins, she mounts

up of her own lightness and flies towards her goal
(*Purg.* XXI, 58–66).

The last pain of all is to pass through fire (Canto
XXVII). This is the stage of purification that pre-
sents the simplest and the most profound allegory.
In speaking of purification by spiritual fire, St.
John of the Cross says: "To comprehend it we must
bear in mind that this fire of Love, before it penetrates the inner parts of the soul, hurts her con-
stantly while it is destroying and consuming away
the weaknesses which come from habitual imper-
fections. By so doing the Holy Ghost disposes the
soul to unite with God and to transform herself by
love into Him. The fire that unites with the soul
in the glory of love, is the same that had beforehand
encompassed her about in order to purify her. It
may be likened to the fire that has entered into the
wood which it destroys. It began by springing upon
it and hurting it by its flames; then it dried it up
and expelled all substances that could prevent it
from burning; and at last, it so wrought upon it by
its heat that it could enter deep into the wood and
transform it into itself" (*The Living Fire of Love*,
Strophe I).

A doubting spirit like Amiel says: "*Toujours et
partout le salut est une torture* (*The Spirit of Man*,
No. 280). But a believer like Saint Gertrude prays:
"Cleanse my soul by fire from all the impurities of
sin, so that it may be rendered capable of receiving
the living flame of thy doctrines, O Lord, and that
Thy Holy Spirit, source of righteousness, may dwell
as a King in all parts of my soul" (*Fifth Exercise*).

These, then, are the four great spiritual aids —
Effort, Prayer, Divine Grace, and Pain — by which
the soul, eager to be good, is enabled to root out the
lower elements of self, vicious habits, base passions,
loose desires, and to establish the Kingdom of
Heaven within.

Dante himself, when he hears the voice of an
angel say that they may not go farther on unless
they first pass through the fire, draws back. Virgil
tries to rouse his courage, but Dante stands immovable before the wall of flame, in stubborn fear. Then
Virgil says:

> Or vedi, figlio,
> tra Beatrice e te è questo muro.

> Now, look, my son,
> Between Beatrice and you is yonder wall.
>
> *Purg.* XXVII, 35–36

and adds, smiling,

> Come?
> volemci star di qua?

> What?
> Do we wish to stay upon this side?
>
> *Ib.* 43–44

At this Dante enters the fire, and Virgil, to distract
his mind, goes on talking of Beatrice, saying:

> Gli occhi suoi già veder parmi.

> Already I seem to see her eyes.
>
> *Ib.* 54

So they passed through the flames and again climbed
upward; but night coming on they are forced to lie

down, on the stairway where they are, and Dante
goes to sleep. When he awakes in the morning, they
climb to the top of the stairs. And now the task of
Human Reason is finished. It has led the pilgrim
to the Earthly Paradise, where the soul is innocent,
and from this time forward, its guide will be Divine
Revelation. So Virgil says:

> Il temporal foco e l'eterno
> veduto hai, figlio, e sei venuto in parte
> dov' io per me più oltre non discerno.
> Tratto t' ho qui con ingegno e con arte;
> lo tuo piacere omai prendi per duce:
> fuor sei dell' erte vie, fuor sei dell' arte.
>
> .   .   .   .
>
> Non aspettar mio dir più, nè mio cenno.
> Libero, dritto e sano è tuo arbitrio,
> e fallo fora non fare a suo senno:
> per ch' io te sopra te corono e mitrio.

> The temporal fire and the eternal,
> Thou hast seen, my Son, and art come there
> Where, of myself, I see my way no more.
> Here have I led thee, in discipline and reason;
> Thy own good pleasure, from now on, take as guide:
> Out of the steep ways, out of the strait ways, art thou now.
>
> .   .   .   .
>
> No more expect a word or sign from me.
> Your will is upright, sound and free,
> And not to follow it would be a wrong.
> Wherefore I crown thee king and do ordain thee priest over
> thyself.

Ib. 127–142

The long task is done, the Mount of Purgatory
has been climbed, and the soul is now pure-eyed
and fit to be led by that human love which has be-

come the truest manifestation of divine holiness,
into an abiding consciousness of the presence of God,

> puro e disposto a salire alle stelle

> pure and ready to mount up to the stars.

Ib. XXXIII, 145

There are many powers at work to help the penitent on his purgatorial way. Dante lays stress on
some. Wordsworth says:

> Here then we rest; not fearing for our creed
> The worst that human reasoning can achieve,
> To unsettle or perplex it; yet with pain
> Acknowledging, and grievous self-reproach,
> That, though immovably convinced, we want
> Zeal, and the virtue to exist by faith
> As soldiers live by courage.

> .   .   .   .

>   What then remains? — To seek
> Those helps for his occasions ever near
> Who lacks not will to use them; vows, renewed
> On the first motion of a holy thought;
> Vigils of contemplation; praise; and prayer, —
> A stream, which from the fountain of the heart
> Issuing, however feebly, nowhere flows
> Without access of unexpected strength.
> But, above all, the victory is most sure
> For him, who, seeking faith by virtue, strives
> To yield entire submission to the law
> Of conscience, — conscience reverenced and obeyed,
> As God's most intimate presence in the soul,
> And his most perfect image in the world,
> — Endeavor thus to live; these rules regard;
> These helps solicit; and a steadfast seat
> Shall then be yours among the happy few
> Who dwell on earth, yet breathe empyreal air,
> Sons of the morning.

The Excursion, Book IV

CHAPTER X

THE HAPPY SIDE OF PURGATORY

IN general it is a consciousness of sin that brings a man face to face with the problem of good and evil; and consciousness of sin is started by some powerful emotion which sweeps in a flood over the ordinary paths of thought and action, and obliterates them quite. Perhaps it is a vision, or an escape from death, or the loss of a child, or the love of a maiden who lives forever in a heaven of memory from which no familiarity can drag her down; some potent cause turns the mind in upon itself to contemplate the beauty of goodness and the ugliness of sin, to wonder why goodness is beautiful and sin ugly, and what they have to do with those powers that move the stars, make flowers grow and build up all the pageant of this perceptible universe, till by degrees the mind, passing on from thought to thought, constructs a philosophy of life, and then persuades the will to bring conduct into accord with that philosophy.

To enter upon this stage is to pass into the gate of Purgatory, for Purgatory is the process of bringing conduct into conformity with a belief in goodness. It is with this stage that Dante the preacher mainly concerns himself. In his letter to Can Grande he says: "The branch of philosophy that regulates [the *Commedia*] in its whole and in its parts, is ethical, because the whole poem was undertaken not for speculation but for practical results" (*Epistola* X, lines 271–275); and it is the *Purgatorio* that depicts how to attain these practical results. The *Inferno* is a picture of life at its lowest, a warning cry, a call to repentance; the "Preacher of Justice" denounces the horrors and loathsomeness of sin, so that we all may profit by his denunciations. And on the other hand, in the *Paradiso* he sets forth the state of those who have entered into the consciousness of the presence of God, in the hope that the picture of their blessedness shall draw men from sin to righteousness. Regarded as an ethical poem, therefore, the whole *Commedia* — *Inferno* and *Paradiso*, as well as the *Purgatorio* — is written for those men and women who, weary and ashamed of days misspent, desire to live a spiritual life, and climb the Hill of Purgatory. And as this world, for the vast majority of people, is neither a Hell nor a Paradise, but a place where hope and purpose struggle with sin, Dante's *Purgatorio* is a far more human place than Hell below or Paradise above, and, in so far as we are concerned with ourselves and our moral well-being, interests us more than either of them does. Hell, the death of the soul, frightens us; we will not voluntarily contemplate it; and Paradise, the ecstasy of conscious union with God, as told by the mystics, if not incomprehensible to the workaday intellect, lies beyond the habitual range of our sympathy. But ordinary human life, the drama of existence, the effort to win in the great wrestling match with low appetites and unworthy desires, appeals to us all. Dante is keenly sensible of this, and therefore, in the *Purgatorio*, so far as is consistent with the whole scheme of the poem, he introduces the characteristic pattern of human life, not only the suffering in it, but also, in generous measure, its happiness and joy,—converse with friends, delight in nature, in the rising and going down of the sun, in birds, in music, in singing, painting, and poetry, in youth and beauty. Rightly to understand the *Purgatorio* the reader must appreciate that Dante (terrible in his prophetic mood when he is denouncing sin, and transcendental in his poetic idealism when he foresees the realization of the command, "Enter thou into the joy of thy Lord") in the *Purgatorio* is human with the common appetite for human happiness and for all pleasures that ennoble men.

The function of Purgatory in human life is to free us from the bondage of sin, and it is therefore of necessity a painful process. Dante never attempts to dodge this truth, but he seeks to impress upon us that this process has a double aspect. Under one aspect, the purification burns out the corruption of the heart as with a hot iron; under the other, the selfsame act unfolds the bandage from the eyes and shows us the more delicate, the more abiding pleasures of life. He will not have us misjudge Purgatory as a place where purification is wrought only by pain, but repeats again and again that purification is also wrought, quite as much, by the refining influences of beauty, of affection, of spiritual insight. Pain we must face, but Pain is fulfilling the office of

Love, and brings its blessing with it. Even while he
describes the sufferings in Purgatory, he exclaims:

> Non vo' però, lettor, che tu ti smaghi
>   di buon proponimento, per udire
>   come Dio vuol che il debito si paghi.
> Non attender la forma del martire;
>   pensa la succession:

> Reader I do not wish to frighten you
>   From good resolves, by hearing how God wills
>   Your trespass must be paid.
> Heed not the nature of the suffering,
>   Think of what lies beyond.
>
> *Purg.* X, 106–110

And he is most solicitous to show us the tender
aspect of the purifying process, and how pregnant
with meaning life appears to the senses that are
being washed clean, as if the world had been made
young and innocent, and the Sons of God again were
shouting for joy. For instance, each hour of day,
morning, or evening has its peculiar and tender
charm:

> Nell' ora che comincia i tristi lai
>   la rondinella,

> At the hour when her sorrowful song
>   The swallow begins;
>
> *Purg.* IX, 13–14

> Era già l'ora che volge il disio
>   ai naviganti, e intenerisce il core
>   lo dì ch' han detto ai dolci amici addio;
> E che lo nuovo peregrin d' amore
>   punge, se ode squilla di lontano,
>   che paia il giorno pianger che si more:

It was the hour when those who sail the sea,
  (The day that they have bid dear friends good-bye)
Feel homeward yearnings and a softer heart,
And when the traveller, just starting on
  His way, is stabbed with pangs of love, if from afar
He hears the bells that seem to weep the dying day.

Ib. VIII, 1–6

And no preacher, since the story of the New Testament, who has taught men to turn towards things of the spirit, not even St. Francis of Assisi, was ever more dextrous and delicate in preaching that goodness brings its own reward. The worst horrors of Hell consist in the hatred sinners feel for one another, with their cursings and mutual wrath; but in Purgatory, the moment the penitent soul perceives the shining of the divine light, even before climbing the purifying ascent itself, she feels the manifestation of God in human friendship, in music, and in poetry. Almost immediately after the poets have emerged from the path leading out of Hell, while still by the shore of the encircling sea, Dante meets his old friend Casella, the musician, a fellow townsman, who had set Dante's odes to music, and the two rush into each other's arms with great affection. And Dante says to him:

Se nuova legge non ti toglie
  memoria o uso all' amoroso canto,
  che mi solea quetar tutte mie voglie,
di ciò ti piaccia consolare alquanto
  l'anima mia, che, con la sua persona
  venendo qui, è affannata tanto

> If new laws do not take from you
> Memory or skill for songs of love
> That used to tranquillize all my desires,
> Please cheer my soul with them awhile,
> Which traveling in its mortal body here
> Is very tired.
>
> *Ib.* II, 106–11

Casella at once begins to sing Dante's ode:

> Amor, che nella mente mi ragiona
> Della mia donna disiosamente,
> Move cose di lei meco sovente
> Che l' intelletto sovr' esse disvia.

> Love, that discourses to me in my mind
> About my Lady lovingly,
> Starts thoughts about her in me oftentimes,
> Mid which my intellect loses its way.
>
> *Canzone* III

Virgil, Dante, and all the company are so charmed by his singing that they stand still for pleasure and quite forget the duty before them, which is to find the ascent towards God.

And further on, there are elaborate episodes that deal with poetry. In one place Dante meets a poet from Lucca, Bonagiunta, an adherent to a conventional, old-fashioned mode of writing poetry, who recognizes him and asks if it is not he that wrote the famous ode in the *Vita Nuova*,

> Donne, ch' avete intelletto d'amore,
> Io vo' con voi della mia donna dire;
> Non perch' io creda sue laude finire,
> Ma ragionar per isfogar la mente.

> Ladies, that have intelligence in love,
>   Of mine own lady I would speak with you;
>   Not that I hope to count her praises through,
>   But telling what I may, to ease my mind.

D. G. Rossetti

It is obvious that Bonagiunta, as he asks the question, is puzzled by the difference between Dante's way of writing verses and his own, which was the way of the older schools, presided over by Jacopo da Lentino (the Notary), and by Guittone d' Arezzo. Dante replies:

> Io mi son un che, quando
>   amor mi spira, noto, ed a quel modo
>   che ditta dentro, vo significando

> I am one who, when
>   Love breathes within me, mark, and in the way
>   He sings to me, I go proclaiming.

And Bonagiunta answers:

> " O frate, issa veggio," disse, "il nodo
>   che il Notaro, e Guittone e me ritenne
>   di qua dal dolce stil nuovo ch' i' odo.
> Io veggio ben come le vostre penne
>   di retro al dittator sen vanno strette,
>   che delle nostre certo non avenne."

> "O brother, now I see," said he, "the knot
>   That held the Notary, Guittone and myself,
>   Back from that sweet, new style I hear.
> And I see well how your pens follow close
>   Behind the Singer, which with us in truth
>   Was not the case."

Purg. XXIV, 52–60

Again and again, Dante intimates that poetry is not only a means of purifying the soul, but also of bringing pleasure to her, and that the purer she becomes the greater is her pleasure. Besides meeting Casella and Bonagiunta, he also meets Guido Guinizelli, the most distinguished of the earlier generation of poets, and Arnaut Daniel, the Provençal, as well (Canto XXVI); and, for a good stretch of the way, Sordello accompanies him (Cantos VI–VIII) and afterwards Statius, the late Latin poet (Cantos XXI–XXVII). No episode is more charming than the meeting with Sordello. This poet is the famous Italian troubadour, who, like Virgil, was born at Mantua.

While Dante and Virgil are still wandering in ante-Purgatory they behold a noble figure standing alone in quiet dignity, looking about him like a lion. Virgil, with no suspicion of who he is, draws near and asks him the best way up the mountain. The stranger does not answer the question, but asks of what country they are. Virgil no sooner begins, "From Mantua —" than the other leaps toward him and cries: "From Mantua you! I am Sordello of your city!" And they hug one another (*Purg.* VI). Then Sordello asks, "Who are you?" and Virgil answers, "*Io son Virgilio*" — "I am Virgil." Sordello stares in sudden bewilderment, then bends and clasps his knees:

> "O gloria de' Latin," disse, "per cui
>   mostrò ciò che potea la lingua nostra,
>   o pregio eterno del loco ond' io fui,
> Qual merito o qual grazia mi ti mostra? "

"O glory of the Latin race," said he, "through whom
    Our language showed what it could do,
    O everlasting honor of my native place!
What merit or what grace shows you to me?"

Purg. VII, 16–19

Just what spiritual refreshment a pilgrim could get
from Sordello or from Statius, I must leave to scholars familiar with their writings; but as it was accepted doctrine that the function of poetry is to
uplift the soul, these poets may be regarded as
symbols, taken somewhat arbitrarily to mean for
readers of that time what Wordsworth, Browning,
Matthew Arnold, Francis Thomson, and many
another, not to mention Dante himself, mean to the
pilgrim to-day.

This friendly intercourse between various persons
on their upward way is perhaps the most noticeable
of the pleasures in Purgatory; but everywhere we
perceive the light of the divine illumination. Sin, even
pride, seen in that light, no longer calls forth our
indignation, but our compassion; and how beautiful
is the description of Humility:

A noi venia la creatura bella,
    bianco vestita, e nella faccia quale
    par tremolando mattutina stella.

Toward us the beauteous creature came
    All robed in white, and in his countenance
    Such as the tremulous morning star.

Purg. XII, 88–90

In fact Purgatory seems far more of a school than
a house of punishment, and goodness is inculcated

by exhortation and precept almost more than by
pains. Virgil, who plays the schoolmaster, says:

> Chiamavi il cielo, e intorno vi si gira,
>   mostrandovi le sue bellezze eterne,
>   e l'occhio vostro pure a terra mira;
>
> The Heavens call you, and whirl around you,
>   Displaying to you their eternal beauty,
>   But your eyes gaze upon the earth.
>
> *Ib.* XIV, 148–150

The pains are grim enough — crushing weights, eyelids sewn up, choking fog, fire — but over and above,
like a flight of bobolinks singing and fluttering in a
radiant sky, flash and echo sights and sounds of
spiritual joy, presentiments of the Earthly Paradise
that lies at the end of the journey. That Earthly
Paradise, of course, is the complete innocence of
the soul, which Wordsworth conceives as the fulfillment of duty:

> Serene will be our days and bright,
> And happy will our nature be,
> When love is an unerring light,
> And joy its own security.

But we are not left with a didactic eulogy of innocence. On the contrary, Dante's picture of it merely
embodies the joy of life. The most perfect simile for
innocence and goodness was when Christ took the
little children and said, "Of such is the kingdom of
Heaven." But since then (one may boldly affirm)
there has been no more charming glimpse of life
unspotted by the world than this of Dante's. He has

reached the river Lethe in the wonderful garden at
the top of Purgatory, and looks across:

e là m'apparve, sì com' egli appare
   subitamente cosa che disvia
   per maraviglia tutt' altro pensare,
una donna soletta, che si gia
   cantando ed iscegliendo fior da fiore,
   ond' era pinta tutta la sua via.
"Deh, bella donna, ch' ai raggi d'amore
   ti scaldi, s'io vo' credere ai sembianti
   che soglion esser testimon del core,
Vegnati voglia di trarreti avanti,"
   diss' io a lei, "verso questa riviera,
   tanto ch' io possa intender che tu canti.
Tu mi fai rimembrar, dove e qual era
   Proserpina nel tempo che perdette
   la madre lei, ed ella primavera."
Come si volge, con le piante strette
   a terra ed intra se, donna che balli,
   e piede innanzi piede a pena mette,
volsesi in sui vermigli ed in sui gialli
   fioretti verso me, non altrimenti
   che vergine che gli occhi onesti avvalli;
e fece i preghi miei esser contenti,
   sì appressando sè, che il dolce suono
   veniva a me co' suoi intendimenti.
Tosto che fu là dove l'erbe sono
   bagnate già dall' onde del bel fiume,
   di levar gli occhi suoi mi fece dono.
Non credo che splendesse tanto lume
   sotto le ciglia a Venere trafitta
   dal figlio, fuor di tutto suo costume.

And there appeared to me — even as doth appear
   Some sudden thing that banisheth
   In wonderment all thoughts of other things —
A lady all alone, who singing went
   And picking flower on flower, with which
   Her path was colored all the way.

"O Lovely Lady, who doth warm thyself
   Beneath the rays of love (if I may credence give
   To looks that often are a witness of the heart)
May thy good will thee nearer bring," said I
   To her, "towards the river bank, so close
   That I may hear the song thou sings't.
Thou bringest to my mind Proserpina,
   Both where and what she was, that time
   Her mother lost her, and she lost the spring."
She turned upon her red and yellow flowers
   Toward me, in just the way a maiden turns
   And drops her modest eyes,
And satisfied my prayers.   She drew so close
   That with her music came to me
   The meaning of her words.
So soon as she was where the grasses bathe
   Within the waters of the lovely stream,
   She granted me a boon — she raised her eyes.
I do not think that ever so much light
   Flashed under Venus' lids, when pierced
   By her son's arrow shot with unwonted force.

                    Purg. XXVIII, 37–66

This lovely lady explains to Dante the nature of
the Earthly Paradise, and singing, "Blessed are they
whose sins are forgiven them," conducts him to where
he shall see Beatrice. The allegory is simple; after
the soul has become as a young child, it is endowed
with heavenly wisdom and is able to understand the
exquisite beauty of innocence. So Milton says:

   That when a soul is found sincerely so,
   A thousand liveried angels lackey her,
   Driving far off each thing of sin and guilt,
   And in clear dream, and solemn vision,
   Tell her of things that no gross ear can hear,
   Till oft converse with heav'nly habitants
   Begin to cast a beam on th' outward shape,

> The unpolluted temple of the mind,
> And turns it by degrees to the soul's essence
> Till all be made immortal.

And Milton's contemporary, George Fox, tells his experience of the Earthly Paradise on the further side of Purgatory in this way: "Now I was come up in spirit through the flaming sword, into the Paradise of God. All things were new; and all creation gave unto me another smell than before, beyond what words can utter. I knew nothing but pureness and innocency, and righteousness, being renewed into the image of God by Christ Jesus, to the state of Adam which he was in before he fell" (*Journal*, 1648).

But the seeker must not expect to find that there is only one road up the Hill of Purgatory, for there are many — a separate road for each it may be. Some may have a path of sorrow, some a path of joy; some may find the road in cloistered ways far from the rush of life, others may find it in the very thick of the struggle.

Pascal prayed: "*Je ne demande pas d'être exempt des douleurs, . . . mais je demande de n'être pas abandonné aux douleurs de la nature sans les consolations de votre esprit.*"[1] It is for the sake of such petitioners that Dante insists that these divine consolations — music, poetry, affection, and visions angelical — are always to be found by the soul that is climbing the road, even the road of pain, to the garden of innocence. Brother Lawrence says "that we must be faithful in doing our duty and denying

[1] Quoted in *The Spirit of Man*, No. 258.

ourselves, and that after that unspeakable pleasures will follow" (*Third Conversation*). And Plato bore his testimony long ago: "He who has been instructed thus far in the science of Love, and has been led to see beautiful things in their due order and rank, when he comes toward the end of his discipline, will suddenly catch sight of a wondrous thing, beautiful with the absolute Beauty; . . . he will see a Beauty eternal, not growing or decaying, not waxing or waning; nor will it be fair here and foul there, nor depending on time or circumstance or place, as if fair to some, and foul to others: . . . Beauty absolute, separate, simple and everlasting; which lending of its virtue to all beautiful things that we see born to decay, itself suffers neither increase nor diminution, nor any other change.

"When a man proceeding onwards from terrestrial things by the right way of loving, once comes to sight of that Beauty, he is not far from his goal. And this is the right way wherein he should go or be guided in his love: he should begin by loving earthly things for the sake of the absolute loveliness, ascending to that as it were by degrees or steps, from the first to the second, and thence to all fair forms; and from fair forms to fair conduct, and from fair conduct to fair principles, until from fair principles he finally arrive at the ultimate principle of all, and learn what absolute Beauty is.

"This life, my dear Socrates, said Diotima, if any life at all is worth living, is the life that a man should live, in the contemplation of absolute Beauty: . . . What if a man's eyes were awake to the sight of the

true Beauty, the divine Beauty, pure, clear and unalloyed, not clogged with the pollutions of mortality,
and the many colours and varieties of human life?
What if he should hold converse with the true
Beauty, simple and divine?

"O think you? she said, that it would be an
ignoble life for a man to be ever looking thither and
with his proper faculty contemplating the absolute
Beauty, and to be living in its presence? Are you
not rather convinced that he who thus sees Beauty as
only it can be seen, will be specially fortuned? And
that, since he is in contact not with images but realities, he will give birth not to images, but to very
Truth itself? And being thus the parent and nurse
of true virtue it will be his lot to become a friend of
God, and, so far as any man can be, immortal and
absolute" (*Symposium*, translation from *The Spirit
of Man*, No. 37).

Poet and philosopher agree with the Apostle Paul
that "without holiness no man shall see the Lord"
(Heb. xii, 14).

CHAPTER XI

INTRODUCTION TO THE PARADISO

PARADISE is attained when the soul, at every moment and in every place, with the subconscious mind if not with the waking consciousness, is aware of the presence of God. "*Ogni dove in cielo è Paradiso,*" Dante says (*Par.* III, 88–89); every place where God is present is Paradise. To the soul, so aware, the world is filled with splendor, and life is a benediction.

> La gloria di Colui che tutto move
> per l'universo penetra,

> The glory of Him who moveth all things
> Permeates the universe.

Par. I, 1–2

This permeating presence of God is manifested in love. "Love," Dante says, "truly taken and subtly considered, is nought else than a spiritual union of the soul and of the thing beloved" (*Conv.* III, Ch. 2); and Paradise is the union of the soul with God. "*Ipsa est beata vita, gaudere de te, ad te, propter te: ipsa est et non est altra*" — "This is the life of blessedness, to rejoice concerning Thee, toward Thee, and because of Thee; this it is and nothing else" (*St. Aug. Conf.* X, Ch. 22).

This conscious union of the soul with God is, no

129

doubt, an experience confined to the very few. These few we call mystics. They believe that in this life they come face to face with God. This meeting, this union, they delight to speak of as the mystical espousals of the soul with God. Their language is figurative, because, such a union being beyond the common experience of normal man, and language having been framed for the use of normal man, there are no words for it. But though their words may not present definite concepts to the rational mind, they are intelligible to the desirous heart. To the outsider, these mystics appear to fall into two categories. The first category includes those who have had visions which affected the senses themselves, such as St. Paul, who saw the strange light in heaven, St. Augustine, who heard the voice say, "*Tolle, lege*," St. Francis of Assisi, who received stigmata, St. Theresa, Jacob Boehme, and others, who believed that with their human senses they heard and saw God. The second category contains those who seem to have received their mystical experiences rather through the imagination than through the senses, such as Plotinus, St. Bonaventura, Ruysbroeck, Pascal, St. John of the Cross, and many more. And there are other differences; different minds have different experiences, see different aspects of truth, and express themselves according to their individuality; and some concern themselves with the culminating felicity itself, while others speak of the way of approach. As Dante's opinions have much in common with those of saints, mystics, and seers, it may help to understand him if I quote from what certain high-souled men have testified concerning this, the deepest experience in life.

An unknown old 'German writer expresses himself thus: "Some may ask what it is to be a partaker of the Divine Nature, or a Godlike [*vergottet*, literally deified] man? Answer: he who is imbued with or illuminated by the Eternal or Divine Light and inflamed or consumed with Eternal or Divine Love, he is a deified man and a partaker of the Divine Nature."[1] Ruysbroeck, the Belgian, with whom Maeterlinck has made us acquainted, asserts: "When love has carried us above all things, above the light, into the Divine Dark, there we are transformed by the Eternal Word Who is the image of the Father; and as the air is penetrated by the sun, thus we receive in peace the Incomprehensible Light, enfolding us and penetrating us. What is this light, if it be not a contemplation of the Infinite and an intuition of Eternity? We behold that which we are, and we are that which we behold, because our being, without losing anything of its own personality, is united with the Divine Truth which respects all diversity."[2] And the Spanish mystic, St. John of the Cross, in comparing the union of the soul with God to a spiritual marriage, says: "The faculties of the soul have attained so perfect a degree of purity, that her will, in its lower sphere as well as in its higher sphere, is wholly detached from seeking, and also from desire, for aught that is not God. For His sake, of all things else she makes an absolute sacrifice.

[1] *Mysticism.* Evelyn Underhill, p. 500.
[2] *Ib.*, p. 506.

Then, by this spontaneous renouncement, the will
of the soul and the will of God become one and the
same, and God does her the favor to take possession
of her, through this conformity of her will with His,
and He lifts her up to the spiritual espousals. In this
state the soul becomes the bride of the Word, and
the Spouse bestows upon her great and precious
favors" (*The Living Fire of Love*, III, line 3).

Jacob Boehme, a very famous German mystic,
whose doctrines greatly influenced George Fox, de-
clares that: "The only way by which God may be
perceived in His word, His essence, and His will, is
that man arrives at the state of unity with himself,
and that — not merely in his imagination but in his
will — he should leave everything that is his personal self, or that belongs to that self . . . and that
his own self should become as nothing to him. He
must surrender everything . . .; he should kill and
annihilate his self-will, the will that claims . . .
things as its possessions. He should surrender all
this to his Creator, and say with the full consent of
his heart, Lord, all is Thine. . . . Act through me
in what manner You will, so that Thy will shall be
done in all things, and that all that I am called upon
to do may be done for the benefit of my brothers,
whom I am serving according to Thy command.
He who enters into such a state of supreme resig-
nation enters into divine union with Christ, so that
he sees God Himself. He speaks with God and God
speaks with him, and he thus knows what is the
Word, the Essence, and the Will of God" (*Jacob
Boehme*, by F. Hartmann, pp. 42–43).

These mystics, German, Belgian and Spanish, use the language of ancient piety, but the meaning is clear. It is stated in modern language by the psychologist, M. Delacroix: "The beginning of the mystic life introduced into the personal life of the subject a group of states [of mind] which are distinguished by certain characteristics, and which form, so to speak, a special psychological system. At its term [end], it has, as it were, suppressed the ordinary self, and by the development of this new system has established a new personality, with a new method of feeling and of action. Its growth results in the transformation of personality; it abolishes the primitive consciousness of selfhood, and substitutes for it a wider consciousness: the total disappearance of selfhood in the divine, the substitution of a Divine Self for the primitive self" (quoted in *Mysticism*, p. 498).

So far the mystics. They are beyond the range of common experience, and therefore usually beyond the reach of our understanding and our sympathy. But between them and us, other men take their station, who also desire union with the infinite, who believe in love, in spiritual life, in self-sacrifice, in faith, and yet keep their feet upon this prosaic, it may be, but dear and beautiful earth. Perhaps I should not say that Emerson, whom I now quote, keeps his feet on the earth, rather he hovers near it on his golden wings; but his thoughts, although tinged with mysticism, are not wholly out of harmony with the rational atmosphere in which we habitually live. That unity of many powers which the mystics symbolize by "Christ" or "God," he calls the Over-soul.

"That Unity, that Over-soul, within which every man's particular being is contained and made one with all other; that common heart . . . to which all right action is submission; that overpowering reality . . . evermore tends to pass into our thought and hand and become wisdom and virtue and power and beauty. . . . And this deep power in which we exist and whose beatitude is all accessible to us, is not only self-sufficing and perfect in every hour, but the act of seeing and the thing seen, the seer and the spectacle, the subject and the object, are one. . . . Of this pure nature every man is at some time sensible. Language cannot paint it with his colors. It is too subtle. It is undefinable, unmeasurable; but we know that it pervades and contains us. . . . There is no . . . bar or wall in the soul, where man, the effect, ceases, and God, the cause, begins. . . . Ineffable is the union of man and God in every act of the soul. The simplest person who in his integrity worships God, becomes God; yet forever and ever the influx of this better and universal self is new and unsearchable. . . . Behold (the soul) saith, I am born into the great, the universal mind. . . . More and more the surges of everlasting nature enter into me. . . . So come I to live in thoughts and act with energies which are immortal" (*The Over-soul*).

Finally, I quote Tolstoi, who stands with his two feet firm on the ground. He does not seek religion in some remote sphere of ecstatic speculation, but in humdrum daily life. He says: "My mistake lay

in ever expecting an examination of finite things to
supply a meaning to life. The finite has no ultimate
meaning apart from the infinite. The two must be
linked together before an answer to life's problems
can be reached. . . . What am I? A part of the infinite. In these few words lies the whole problem"
(*My Confession*).

Such are the beliefs of some spiritual minds seeking to comprehend the relation of the finite with the
infinite, of man's soul with God, and they shed some
light for us when we are speculating as to what may
be the meaning of those phrases employed by the
saints, such as "the state of blessedness," "the
Paradise of the elect," "the Kingdom of Heaven."

In the *Paradiso* Dante expounds his beliefs; he
uses the language, the phrases, the metaphors of his
time, and these are very rich and magnificent; nevertheless under all the splendor of poetical imagining
the human structure of his beliefs, as they apply
to earthly life, may be discerned. If my interpretation
is dogmatic, it is for simplicity's sake. The *Divine
Comedy* is like a forest of truth in which a thousand
men can climb a thousand trees, and each man, as
he mounts nearer toward heaven, fondly believes
that he has chosen the poet's tree of life. Dante, then,
whatever he may say to learned men, says this to
the simple: Paradise is within our own souls, and to
dwell in Paradise, means to be sensitive to the hal-
lowing influences of life, to fix our eyes upon the
beauty of holiness, as the lover gazes up at the window in which his lady shall appear; it means, to
tend and watch over — as April with its sunshine

and its rain tends and watches over the "rathe primrose" — our uncertain and tremulous hope that the power which moves throughout the universe, and impels all motions, may best be interpreted to men by its manifestation in that love which St. Paul describes; it means the conviction that man is of one substance with all the universe, that he and it have a common purpose, a common task, and a common destiny, that this consubstantiality is of soul and mind, as well as of body, and that universal harmony is necessary for universal joy.

Dante, like ourselves, cannot explain why the joy of harmony does not prevail throughout the universe. Something is wrong; the stuff out of which men are made, we do not know why, does not take the shape divine influence would impress upon it (*Par.* XIII, 67–69, and I, 127–129). But that seeming misfortune is our good fortune in disguise. Life would lose its highest incentive, and love of God have little meaning, if we had no task to perform, if we could not aspire to be His agents to do His work. In Purgatory our duty is to renounce and to purify; in Paradise it is to gratify the deep religious instinct of the human heart. "Nearer, my God, to Thee" — that is the subject of the *Paradiso*. Beatrice, an emanation from God, conducts the innocent soul up from plane to plane, until the heart, mind, and soul attain "the complete and perfect possession of unlimited life at a single moment" (Boethius, quoted by Gardner, *Dante and the Mystics*, p. 28).

This approach nearer and nearer to God, the *navigatio ad patriam* (*Ib.* p. 61), has been the subject

of dearest interest to the mystics. Plotinus, the
Neoplatonic philosopher of Alexandria, says: "The
first thing is to render the organ of vision analogous
and similar to the object which it is to contemplate.
The eye could never have perceived the sun, if it had
not first taken the form of the sun; in the same way,
the soul could never see beauty, if she were not first
beautiful herself, and every man must begin by
making himself beautiful and divine in order to
obtain sight of what is beautiful and divine" (quoted
by Maeterlinck, *Ruysbroeck l'admirable*). And St.
Bonaventura says of this drawing near: "But if thou
wouldst know how these things are done, question
grace, not doctrine; desire, not understanding; the
sob of prayer, not the study of texts; the bridegroom,
not the master; God, not man; darkness, not clarity;
not light, but the fire that inflames utterly and
transfers into God, with excessive fervour and most
ardent love" (*Dante and the Mystics*, p. 253).

But for this drawing near we must remember
that God is Truth as well as that God is Love, and
therefore that the way of approach must be by the
intellect as well as by the heart. God — the Absolute,
the Real, the Infinite, Matter, Motion, Mind, Spirit,
call Him by what name you will — is beyond the
reach of the human intellect; nevertheless seekers
believe, or at least they hope, that all things which
exist contribute in some measure towards a knowledge of God. The laws by which the stars move and
"perform their shining," the principles of chemistry,
the manifestations of electricity, the habits of
animals, the yearnings of man, the brain of Newton,

the imagination of Shakespeare, the compassion of Jesus, each and all bring their candles and help us see a little, however minute that little is in comparison with the unmeasured bulk of our ignorance, and give us the hope that by this candle light we may see the path on which we may walk in accordance with His will.

Dante, one might almost say, was more interested in the intellect than in the heart. He studied all the religious philosophy of his time, and would not have us think ourselves safe in following an undisciplined, uninstructed conscience. To know the right is, according to him, a matter that will tax the profoundest thinkers. God, it is said, does not make Himself manifest to cowards; neither does He make Himself manifest to the slothful or the blind. Dante would have us study William James, Bergson, Eucken, James Martineau, and all thinkers who have pondered upon the means of coming nearer to the goal of all desire. It is, nevertheless, not easy to explain the theory of the road to God by the intellect, as Dante understood it, so that it shall be serviceable to us to-day. The best way to make it intelligible, and possibly serviceable, will be to cite what St. Augustine says concerning it, and therefore I cite an extract from his *Confessions*, Book IX, Ch. 10. "The day was now approaching that [my mother Monica] was to depart this life, . . . and it befell, as I believe, because Thou brought it about by Thy secret ways, that she and I were standing by ourselves leaning against a certain window which looked out on the garden enclosed by the house in which we were, at Ostia on the Tiber; and there, sequestered from the company, after the fatigue of a long journey, we were recruiting our strength for the sea voyage. So, we were talking together, alone, very sweetly, and forgetting those things which are behind and reaching forth unto those things that are before, and we were inquiring of one another (by considering the Present Truth, which Thou art), what would be the eternal life of the saints, which eye hath not seen nor ear heard, neither hath it entered into the heart of man. And we panted in the thirstiness of our hearts for the upper waters of Thy fountain, the fountain of life that is in Thee; so that, besprinkled with it, according to our capacity, we might in some sort meditate on so high a matter. And when our discourse was once come to the point that the greatest pleasure of the bodily senses, in their greatest material glitter, contrasted with the joy of that life, was to the seeing eye not merely not worthy of comparison, but not even of mention. And being lifted up by a more burning affection toward that life, we by degrees passed beyond all material things, even the sky, from which sun, moon and stars shine upon the earth. Thither we ascended, inwardly musing, discoursing, and wondering at Thy works, and we passed on to our minds, and transcended mind, until we touched the region of riches that never fail . . . where life is that Wisdom, by which all things are made, both those that have been and those that are to be. (This wisdom is not made, but it is now as it has been and ever shall be. Nay, indeed, the terms 'to have been' and 'shall be' do not belong to it, but only the term 'I am,' since it is everlasting. For to eternity there is neither past nor future.) And while we talked and panted for it, by the impulsion of our whole heart, we attained in a meagre measure to the edge of it. . . . So we said: Suppose that the tumult of the flesh be silent, that the phantasms of earth and waters and air be silent, that the heavens be silent and the soul itself be silent, and by not thinking of itself transcend self; suppose, that dreams be silent and the fantasies of the imagination, that every tongue, and every sign, and that whatever is in course of creation be altogether silent — since if any one should hearken to them, all things say, 'We have not made us but He who abides forever made us'; and suppose that having uttered this they also are silent (for they have lifted up our ears to Him who made them), and suppose that He Himself speaks alone, not by His creatures, but of Himself, so that we hear His own word, not by tongue of flesh, nor by voice of angel, nor by the sound of thunder, nor by the riddle of allegory, but hear Him Himself, whom manifested in these, His creatures, we love, Himself without them (just as now we stretch forth and in swift thought touch the eternal wisdom that abides over all); suppose this exultation of spirit continue and all other visions of wholly inferior kind be taken away, and this one vision ravish the beholder, swallow him up, and immerse him in these inward joys, and suppose that his life were to be forever like to this moment of understanding for which we have been sighing, is not this the benediction: 'Enter thou into the joy of thy Lord'?"

For St. Augustine the great spiritual adventure of personal consciousness of the presence of God is primarily intellectual, and so I think it was with Dante; but with others (and these are the far larger number) it is primarily emotional, manifesting itself in a passionate desire for nearness to God. Nowadays (I speak of the time before the war), at least in our industrial society, the love of God, however glib upon the lips, is a pale, languid, tepid emotion, compared with the fiery passion of the mediaeval Catholic saints. But to understand the *Paradiso* we must feel, behind the scholastic expositions that occur somewhat frequently, this white heat of love, and to that end I quote from St. Gertrude and from Dante's countrywoman, St. Catherine of Siena.

St. Gertrude expresses herself in this way: "I come, I come toward Thee, O loving Jesus! Toward Thee whom I have loved, whom I have sought, whom I have longed for. Drawn by Thy gentleness, by Thy compassion, by Thy charity, I give myself up at Thy call, loving Thee with all my heart, with all my soul, with all my might. Let me not be confounded in my hope, but deal with me according to Thy gentleness and according to the magnitude of Thy mercy. . . . Holy Ghost! Love! Love! Tell me the way that leadeth to so delightful an abiding-place, and where the path of life is that leadeth to those fields fruitful from the dew divine, at which thirsty souls slake their thirst. O Love, Thou alone knowest the way that leads to life and truth. . . . By Thee, O Holy Ghost, are the best gifts poured upon us; from Thee proceed the fruitful seeds which bring forth the fruits of life; from Thee emanates the sweet honey of the delights that exist only in God; from Thee descend upon us the fertilizing waters of the blessings of the Lord of hosts, the dear, rare gift of the Spirit" (*Third Exercise*).

And St. Catherine of Siena, in describing the love of the soul for God, says: "The soul, that already perceiveth her own nothingness, and knoweth that all her good lies in the Creator, abandons herself and all her faculties, and all created things, and immerses herself wholly in her Creator, so that she directs all her workings wholly toward Him, and will not depart at any point from Him, in whom she is aware she has found all good and all perfection of happiness; and from this union of love, which increases in her day by day, the soul so transforms herself in a certain manner into God that she cannot think, nor purpose, nor love aught except God, nor can she remember aught else but God, and she perceiveth neither self nor created thing except in God, and remembereth neither self nor created thing save only in Him; just as a man who sinks in the sea and swims beneath its waters, neither sees nor touches aught but the waters of the sea and things that are in the water, and neither sees, nor touches, nor feels aught that is out of the water" (*La Vita*, Part I, Ch. X, Sec. 8). And of her own passion for God, she says to her confessor: "So great was the fire of the love of God, and of my yearning to unite with Him, whom I loved, that even if my heart had been of stone or of iron, it would have burst asunder in like manner and been opened. No created thing, I believe, could have had the power to preserve my heart whole against such power of love. Therefore take it as certain that the heart of my little body cracked from top to bottom from the very violence of love, and lay all open, so that I still seem to feel the marks of that opening. From this you can clearly gather that my soul was wholly separated from my body and I saw the mysteries of God, which no traveller can tell of, since neither has the memory power, nor can human words suffice, to set forth in proper manner matters so sublime, so that whatever I could say would be as clay when matched with gold" (*Vita*, Part II, Ch. VI, Sec. 21).

A similar state of mind is told of, in a more restrained way, by an American woman, Mrs. Jonathan Edwards. "All night I continued in a constant, clear and lively sense of the heavenly sweetness of Christ's excellent and transcendent love, of his nearness to me, and of my dearness to him; with an inexpressibly sweet calmness of soul in an entire rest in him. I seemed to myself to perceive a glow of divine love come down from the heart of Christ in heaven, into my heart, in a constant stream, like a stream or pencil of sweet light. At the same time my heart and soul all flowed out in love to Christ; so that there seemed to be a constant flowing and reflowing of heavenly and divine love, from Christ's heart to mine; and I appeared to myself to float, or swim, in these bright sweet beams of the sun, or the streams of his light which came in at the window. My soul remained in a kind of heavenly Elysium. . . . It seemed to be all that my feeble frame could sustain, of that fullness of joy, which is felt by those who behold the face of Christ, and share his love in the heavenly world. . . . To my imagination my soul seemed to be gone out of me to God and Christ in heaven, and to have very little relation to my body. God and Christ were so present to me, that I seemed removed from myself. . . . When I arose on the morning of the Sabbath, I felt a love to all mankind, wholly peculiar in its strength and sweetness, far beyond all that I had ever felt before. The power of that love seemed to me inexpressible. I thought, if I were surrounded by enemies, who were venting their malice and cruelty upon me, in tormenting me, it would still be impossible that I should cherish any feelings towards them but those of love, of pity, and ardent desires for their happiness" (Jan. 28–29–30, 1742).

But over and above these two ways, by the intellect and by the heart, of proceeding from the outskirts of Paradise toward the very central point of spiritual gravitation, there is (and Dante fully recognizes it) the mystic way, which is, it would seem, due to the action of grace. The soul, washed and anointed as it were, innocent of earthly stains and yearning for upward flight, of a sudden is rapt on high into the presence of God. The best known experience of this kind is that of St. Paul, who says: "I will come to visions and revelations of the Lord. I knew a man in Christ . . . (whether in the body I cannot tell; or whether out of the body, I cannot tell: God knoweth) such an one caught up to the

third heaven. And I know such a man (whether in
the body or out of the body, I cannot tell: God
knoweth) how that he was caught up into Paradise,
and heard unspeakable words" (II Cor. xii, 1–4).
Dante uses very much the same words in the opening of the *Paradiso:*

> Nel ciel che più della sua luce prende
>   fu' io; e vidi cose che ridire
>   nè sa nè può qual di lassu discende. . . .
> S' io era sol di me quel che creasti
>   novellamente, Amor che il ciel governi,
>   tu il sai, che col tuo lume mi levasti.

> Within the heaven that of His light doth most
>   Receive, was I; and things beheld, that to retell
>   He neither knowledge hath nor power, who thence
> Comes down . . .
> If I was there a bodyless soul
>   In spirit only, Thou knowest, O Love,
>   That in the heavens reignest, for with Thy light
> Thou didst me lift.
>
>

Par. I, 4–6, 73–75

Some people think that, by these words, Dante
means to tell us that he himself had just such a
mystical experience as St. Paul had; others think
that he speaks figuratively, and was rapt to heaven
only in imagination. Whichever it was, Dante shows
his belief in a Power that, of a sudden, after the soul
has become purified, etherealized, hallowed by pain,
effort, prayer, and righteousness, descends like a
ministering angel in a cloud of light, and, lifting her
up, bears her, higher and higher, to the very top of
human blessedness. This belief is set forth at length
in the *Paradiso*.

CHAPTER XII

THE PARADISO

TO the non-philosopher, Paradise is primarily a personal problem; and as such, although it had its universal aspect as well, it presented itself to Dante. The *Paradiso* is his answer to the problem, unfolding the solution in its several stages, as a flower unfolds its encircling petals, opening first the outer envelope, and gradually disclosing row upon row, until at last it lays bare its very heart. From heaven to heaven, the self mounts upward into universal love and truth, but the self is never lost, neither is it diminished, but rises higher and higher, conscious and triumphant.

Taking the narrative in its literal sense, the analogy closest at hand for the reader of to-day, is to the flight of an aëroplane, as aviators describe it. The soul is aware of a sudden motion, it rises from the ground, escaping from the bonds of terrestrial gravitation, and mounts, higher and higher, soaring up into the empyrean, till the earth becomes little more than a memory, and the blue vault of heaven is above and below and all around. But for the allegory this analogy must be pieced out with another. The uprising soul is like a young lover. He sees the object of his love, good and beautiful. His passion, like purgatorial fire, burns away the

146

dross within his heart, and transfuses all his being
with yearning for goodness and beauty; it unlooses
from his eyes the veil of uncharitableness, and shows
him how goodness and beauty are present in all
things,

> How many goodly creatures are there here!
> How beauteous mankind is! O brave new world,
> That has such people in't!

The reason that all the world loves a lover is that
all the world feels the presence of this divine passion, and opens the windows of its spirit to the re-
freshing breath. So the soul in Paradise is in love
and mounting higher and higher; and in every canto
of the *Paradiso*, in almost every line, we are bathed
in the light of love and we hear the beat of soaring
wings.

Nevertheless, this blessedness, in itself the same,
is possessed in varying measure by different persons:

> Differentemente han dolce vita,
> per sentir più e men l'eterno spiro.

> In differing modes do they possess sweet life,
> According as they feel, or more or less, the eternal breath.

> *Par.* IV, 35–36

These differences Dante illustrates by means of the
nine revolving heavens. The Ptolemaic astronomy
seems to have been devised on purpose for a prophet-
poet, so admirable is the allegory it furnishes for
the spiritual interpretation of life. The earth rests
immobile in the center, and round it revolve sphere
after sphere, upon the same axis, first that of the

Moon, then in succession those of Mercury, Venus, the Sun, Mars, Jupiter, Saturn, the Fixed Stars, and the Primum Mobile. In these spheres appear souls of different categories. And these different categories exist, because even in heaven the soul cannot free herself from the mold in which she has been cast by the experience of life; even in the presence of God we do not lose our personality. Dante all the time reiterates the lesson, that in making our characters we are building everlastingly, for better or worse. Souls that have been dented by sin, or stunted in their growth, cannot contain the grace of God in the same brimful measure as souls unspotted by the world. Like the *Inferno* and the *Purgatorio*, the *Paradiso* is the song of a prophet, a passionate lover of righteousness.

In Paradise the first duty of the soul is to submit like a child to the guidance of the highest aspirations that the mind can compass, and this is the guidance of the Wisdom of Love, of Beatrice, the bringer of beatitude. So, in the opening canto, while Beatrice has her eyes fixed on high, Dante fixes his eyes on hers, and he becomes so absorbed in his thought of her that what is left of the unspiritual part of his nature falls away from him, and he is ready for his journey. And since greater knowledge is the stepping stone to the greater love of God, Beatrice instructs him as they go. The first lesson is how love manifests itself in order; for love without peace is not love, and peace without order is not peace. The will of God, which in its application to what our senses report we call the laws of nature, prevails in

beauty everywhere in heaven; and Beatrice, opening Dante's mind to how "the firmament showeth
His handiwork," reveals to him the workings of the
several heavenly spheres and their influences on the
souls and destinies of men, and thereby explains to
him the reason why men are born different and have
different lives.

Dante's own conception of the action of God's
energy in the universe was in accordance with the
scholastic doctrines of his time, and, roughly speaking, after this fashion: "Within the heaven of Divine
Peace," that is, as we may say, within the un-
fathomable, encompassing mind of God, the first
revolving heaven (within which revolve all the lesser
spheres) is vibrant with divine energy; and this
energy, both directed and altered by the medium
through which it passes, proceeds to the inner
spheres, affecting the nearest most, and those more
remote according to their remoteness, and also
affecting all things contained within those spheres
according to their several natures. In like manner
each of the other spheres radiates this energy on-
ward to the spheres within, and to all things within
them, but in diminished measure. This energy is
spiritual; it is as if all the universe were held in the
arms of God and received the pulsations of His
infinite heart. In this way, all parts of the universe,
whatever their form or matter, receive this divine
energy and pass it on; so that, although the source
of all energy, mechanical, vital, mental, spiritual, is
one, the energy manifests itself in a myriad different
ways (*Par.* II).

All the way, either from Beatrice or from the souls they meet, Dante learns the operation of the laws of God. Perhaps the greatest lesson of all he receives in the lowest of the ten heavens, the sphere of the Moon. Here he meets the soul of Piccarda, a Florentine lady, who in life, under compulsion, broke her nun's vow and married, and this unfaithfulness has left its everlasting mark. Dante asks her if she does not desire to be in a higher heaven, in a place of greater glory, where she would be nearer to God. Piccarda smiles, as radiantly as if she were in the rapture of first love, and answers:

> Frate, la nostra volontà quieta
> virtù di carità, che fa volerne
> sol quel ch' avemo, e d'altro non ci asseta.
> Se disiassimo esser più superne,
> foran discordi gli nostri disiri
> dal voler di colui che qui ne cerne,
> che vedrai non capere in questi giri,
> s' essere in caritate è qui *necesse*,
> e se la sua natura ben rimiri.
> Anzi è formale ad esto beato *esse*
> tenersi dentro alla divina voglia,
> per ch' una fensi nostre voglie stesse.
> Sì che, come noi sem di soglia in soglia
> per questo regno, a tutto il regno piace,
> come allo re ch' a suo voler ne invoglia;
> e la sua volontate è nostra pace:

> Brother, the quality of love constrains our will,
> And lets us only wish for what we have,
> And thirst for nothing more.
> If we should wish to be up higher than
> We are, our wills would be at discord
> With His will, who put us here.

And that within these circles cannot be,
   Since to live in Love is here necessity,
   If you consider well Love's nature.
Rather it is the law of this life beatific
   To keep ourselves within the Will Divine,
   So that our several wills shall make but one.
And so, being as we are, from sphere to sphere
   Throughout this realm, gives joy to all the realm,
   And to our King, who makes our wills like His.
And His will is our peace.

Par. III, 70–87

This means that contentment is an essential element in Paradise, although we needed no spirit come back from the realms of the dead to tell us that; and, in like manner, the other spheres indicate other constituent parts of perfect blessedness. In the sphere of Mercury, Dante meets the Emperor Justinian, who inculcates, as the idea appropriate to that sphere, the absence of worldly ambition. In the sphere of Venus Dante learns that, even though tainted by an earthly element, true love brings with it a touch of Paradise. In the next (that of the Sun), St. Thomas Aquinas, by the story of St. Francis of Assisi and Lady Poverty, teaches that the soul, before she can enter Paradise, must be wholly free from material cares; and St. Bonaventura, by the story of St. Dominic, that we must have faith, a faith in some end, whatever it be, a faith that shall justify and consecrate the most complete sacrifice of self. In the heaven of Mars, Dante's ancestor, Cacciaguida, implies that heroism must temper the soul; and in that of Jupiter, the spirits of righteous kings symbolize a state of peace, order, and justice in the soul which desires to establish within herself the kingdom of God.

Next, in the heaven of Saturn, Dante comes to the foot of the Celestial Ladder, which is the stair of ascent towards what the heart holds as best and noblest. This ladder means meditation. It is upon the contemplative mind, meditating on the things of God, that the power and peace of the spirit shed their refreshment, whether that power and peace come direct from God or from the subconscious mind, or from the treasure house of rest — judge it as you please. James Martineau, that modern English saint, says of meditation: "Its view is not personal and particular, but universal and immense. . . . It brings not an intense self-consciousness and spiritual egotism, but almost a renunciation of individuality, a mingling with the universe, a lapse of our little drop of existence into the boundless ocean of being. It does not find for us our place in the known world, but loses it for us in the unknown. It puts nothing clearly beneath our feet, but a vault of awful beauty above our head. It gives us no matter for criticism and doubt, but everything for wonder and love. It does not suggest indirect demonstration, but furnishes immediate perception of things divine, eye to eye with the saints, spirit to spirit with God, peace to peace with Heaven. In thus being alone with the truth of things and passing from shows and shadows into consciousness with the Everlasting One, there is nothing at all impossible and out of reach" (*Endeavours after a Christian Life*, p. 258). And Jonathan Edwards says of his thoughts in a time of meditation: "I walked abroad alone, in a solitary place in my father's pasture, for contemplation. And as I was walking there, and looking upon the sky and clouds, there came into my mind so sweet a sense of the glorious majesty and grace of God, as I know not how to express. I seemed to see them both in a sweet conjunction; majesty and meekness joined together; it was a sweet, and gentle, and holy majesty; and also a majestic sweetness; an awful sweetness; a high, and great, and holy gentleness. After this my sense of divine things gradually increased, and became more and more lively, and had more of that inward sweetness. The appearance of everything was altered; there seemed to be, as it were, a calm, sweet cast, or appearance of divine glory in almost everything. God's excellency, his wisdom, his purity and love, seemed to appear in everything; in the sun, moon, and stars; in the clouds and blue sky; in the grass, flowers, trees; in the water and all nature; which used greatly to fix my mind. I often used to sit and view the moon for a long time; and in the day spent much time in viewing the clouds and sky, to behold the sweet glory of God in these things; in the meantime, singing forth, with a low voice, my contemplations of the Creator and Redeemer."

The exercise of meditation or contemplation—for they merge into one another—procures the fulfillment of the benediction, "May the peace of God which passeth all understanding keep your hearts and minds in the knowledge and love of God"; it fixes the heart and mind on spiritual values, and of neces-

sity discloses the falseness of worldly measures.
So Dante, "*le luce sue chiare ed acute,* his eyes clear
and keen" (*Par.* XXII, 126), looking down from on
high through all the lower spheres, sees our world
and smiling at its obvious worthlessness, says:

> E quel consiglio per migliore approbo
>   che l'ha per meno, e chi ad altro pensa
>   chiamar si può veracemente probo.

> And I esteem that wisdom best
>   Which rates the world at least; and he whose thoughts
>   Are elsewhere fixed, deserves the name of good..
>   *Par.* XXII, 136–8

Having learned to hold the world cheap, the soul
contemplates the spirit of Christ and its effect upon
those who were nearest to Him, Mary and the
Apostles. Then, by such contemplation deepened
and ennobled, the soul seeks to take her own measure,
to know herself, to make essay, by examination of
her deepest beliefs, whether she is capable of still
greater heights and of ultimate union with God. In
the allegory this process is represented by an examination of Dante, as to his faith by St. Peter,
as to his hope by St. James, and as to his love by St.
John. "Faith is the substance of things hoped for,
the evidence of things not seen" (Hebrews xi, 1);
or, as it may be expressed in terms more current
to-day, Faith is the belief in a spiritual order, which
we cannot define, fenced in as we are by corporeal
experience, and yet we think we can judge what road
humanity must travel in order to come into deeper
relations therewith.

Io credo in uno Iddio
solo ed eterno, che tutto il ciel move,
non moto, con amore e con disio.

I believe in one God
Single and everlasting who, Himself unmoved,
Moves all the heaven, by love and longing.

Par. XXIV, 130–132

This dogma means that there is universal unity,
that all things are one, explain their separation,
their discord, their contradictions and antagonisms,
how you will, and that all things seek, by a transcendental law of mutual attraction — which in the
language of the human heart we call love and
longing — to attain to the highest fulfillment of their
potential life, whatever that life may be.

"Hope is the certain expectation of future glory,
and is due to divine grace and antecedent merit."

Speme . . . è uno attender certo
della gloria futura, il qual produce
grazia divina e precedente merto.

Ib. XXV, 67–69

But it does not require Dante's knowledge of theology
to discern that hope is the foundation of religion.
Hope is to men the assurance of a divine compassion;
it blesses the meanest creatures. It is the music that
ushers in belief. It is the watchman on the turret's
top who sees the far-off runner bringing news of
victory. Its vagueness, its amplitude, its confidence,
are so many witnesses to a nobler order in which the
soul of man shall be lifted up. It is certainly brought
forth by grace divine — for it bears the marks of

divine origin; and preceding merit coöperates, for sin which stifles every merit is not a soil that can bring forth such a plant. And with Dante, as with many another man, belief in the highest promises of hope comes from the testimony of great hearts who have had a rich experience of life. For him the words of David, — "They that know Thy name will put their trust in Thee" (Psalm ix, 10) — were of great significance, and also what St. James says in his epistle, partly, perhaps, from the words themselves, and partly because St. James was the familiar friend of Jesus Christ: "My brethren, count it all joy when ye fall into divers temptations; knowing this, that the trying of your faith worketh patience. But let patience have her perfect work, that ye may be perfect and entire, wanting nothing. If any of you lack wisdom, let him ask of God, that giveth to all men liberally, and upbraideth not; and it shall be given him. . . . Blessed is the man that endureth temptation: for when he is tried he shall receive the crown of life. . . . Every good gift and every perfect gift is from above, and cometh down from the Father of lights, with whom is no variableness, neither shadow of turning. Of his own will begat he us with the word of truth, that we should be a kind of first-fruits of his creatures. . . . The wisdom that is from above is first pure, then peaceable, gentle, and easy to be intreated, full of mercy and good fruits, without partiality, and without hypocrisy. . . . Know ye not that the friendship of the world is enmity with God? whosoever therefore will be a friend of the world, is the enemy of God. . . . Draw

nigh to God and he will draw nigh to you. . . .
Humble yourselves in the sight of the Lord, and he
shall lift you up. . . . Is any among you afflicted?
Let him pray" (James, i, iii, iv, v).

As to love, Dante says that God is the object of
all love. He learned this first from philosophic arguments. Good that is recognized as good kindles love,
and the greater the good, the greater the love; therefore Perfect Good must kindle the strongest love;
and this rational reasoning was confirmed by authority, by Aristotle, by the Book of Exodus, — "I
will make all my goodness pass before Thee" (xxxiii,
19) — and by Revelations. Besides this, man's love
for God is due to gratitude for creation of the world
and of himself, and for redemption. Dante puts this
examination and appraisal of Faith, Hope, and
Charity in language most readily intelligible to his
contemporaries, but every man must make them
for himself; and unless he can find a place in his soul
for each of the three, he cannot hope (so Dante says)
to build a Kingdom of Heaven within him.

Thus qualified to go upward, Dante mounts
through the last revolving sphere up to the empyrean, eternal peace, which lying outside the barriers
of time and space, enfolds creation, —

> al ciel, ch' è pura luce;
> luce intelletual piena d'amore,
> amor di vero ben pien di letizia,
> letizia che trascende ogni dolzore;

> the heaven which is pure light;
> Light intellectual filled full of gladness,
> Gladness that doth transcend all sweetness.
>
> *Par.* XXX, 39–42

Lume è lassù, che visible face
lo Creatore a quella creatura,
che solo in lui vedere ha la sua pace;

Up yonder is the light that visible
Makes the Creator to the created soul,
Which only in beholding Him has peace.

Ib. 100–2

The soul has now mounted very high, and is coming
close to the fulfillment of all desire; and as it nears
its Beloved, expectation and desire become intense.
To those who do not know what it is to love, this
passion of the soul is incomprehensible. St. Gertrude
says: "Here I am, coming nearer to Thee, Thou
Devouring Fire, O my God! In the fiery flames of
Thy love devour me, consume me, absorb me, poor
grain of dust. Here am I, coming nearer to Thee, O
my gentle Light! Cause Thy face to shine upon me;
and my darkness shall be in Thy presence as brilliant
as the sun at noon. Here am I, coming nearer to
Thee, O Blessedness! Make me one with Thee, by
that burning love that draws Thee towards Thy
creatures to unite them to Thee" (*Fourth Exercise*).
All the mystics felt as she did. The Empyrean is the
passion of love for God at its height. And here Dante
hardly appeals to what we may ever expect to learn
through experience, but rather to what we may hope
to apprehend through the imagination, by means
of spiritual inferences from earthly love.

In this ultimate heaven Dante, his eyes endued
with superhuman power to bear the sight, stands
before the mystic Rose, whose petals are the souls
triumphant that encircle God. Here Beatrice calls

St. Bernard, and commends Dante to his charge.
St. Bernard is the symbol of mystical contemplation.
The mind, struggling to compass the transcendental,
gazes on some symbol of spirit, as the bodily eyes
gaze on the beryl stone, and beholds visions that in
its normal state it does not see. This supernormal
yearning of the soul seems to burst the bonds of
sense, and escape the limitations of humanity. The
final means is prayer. St. Bernard prays to the Virgin
Mary that Dante may behold God face to face.

The Virgin Mary is the embodiment, or the symbol, of those manifestations of God that stir in us
spiritual feelings which, even in our fallen state,
rank next in power to the primitive animal impulses,
and, when once the purgatorial process has begun
within our souls, lightly triumph over all instincts.
As Virgin, she demands the romantic admiration
for loveliness and the chivalric reverence for purity,
such as young Dante felt when he met Beatrice in
the streets of Florence; as the Madonna, she repre-
sents the compassion, the tender understanding, the
self-abnegation, and the adoration of the mother
for the child, who in turn is the symbol of a higher
life to come. To her St. Bernard prays (*Par.* xxxiii):

> Vergine madre, figlia del tuo figlio,
>   umile ed alta più che creatura,
>   termine fisso d'eterno consiglio,
> tu se' colei, che l'umana natura
>   nobilitasti sì che il suo Fattore
>   non disdegnò di farsi sua fattura.
> Nel ventre tuo si raccese l'amore,
>   per lo cui caldo nell' eterna pace
>   così è germinato questo fiore,

Qui sei a noi meridiana face
   di caritate, e giuso, intra i mortali,
   sei di speranza fontana vivace.
Donna, sei tanto grande e tanto vali,
   che qual vuol grazia ed a te non ricorre,
   sua disianza vuol volar senz' ali.
La tua benignità non pur soccorre
   a chi domanda, ma molte fiate
   liberamente al domandar precorre.

Thou mayde and mooder, doghter of thy sone,
Thou welle of mercy, sinful soules cure,
In whom that God, for bountee, chees to wone; [1]
Thou humble, and heigh over every creature,
Thou nobledest so ferforth our nature,
That no desdayn the maker hadde of kinde, [2]
His son in blode and flesh to clothe and winde.

Withinne the cloistre blisful of thy sydes
Took mannes shap the eternal love and pees,
That of the tryne compas lord and gyde [3] is,
Whom erthe, and see, and heven, out of relees, [4]
Ay herien; [5] and thou, virgine wemmelees, [6]
Bar of thy body, and dweltest maiden pure,
The creatour of every creature.
Assembled in thee magnificence
With mercy, goodnesse, and with swich [7] pitee,
That thou, that art the sonne of excellence,
Nat only helpest hem that preyen thee,
But ofte tyme, of thy benignitee,
Ful frely, er that men thyn help biseche,
Thou goost biforn, and art hir [8] lyves leche. [9]

CHAUCER,   The Seconde Nonnes Tale,
vv. 36–56

---

[1] to dwell.   [2] humanity.
[3] lord and guide of the threefold region.
[4] without ceasing.   [5] always praise.   [6] stainless.
[7] such.   [8] their.   [9] leach (physician).

St. Bernard then points to Dante:

> Or questi, che dall' infima lacuna
> dell' universo infin qui ha vedute
> le vite spiritali ad una ad una,
> supplica a te, per grazia, di virtute
> tanto che possa con gli occhi levarsi
> più alto verso l'ultima salute.

Now this man here, who from the lowest pit
   Of all the universe, even up to here,
   Has seen the lives of spirits, one by one,
Beseeches thee, through grace, for so much power
   That with his eyes he may have strength to look
   Still higher, towards the final blessedness.

Par. XXXIII, 22–27

Mary grants the prayer, and turns her eyes towards God. Then Dante speaks of himself:

> Ed io ch' al fine di tutti i disii
> m' appropinquava, sì com' io dovea,
> l' ardor del desiderio in mi finii;
>
> . . . .
>
> chè la mia vista, venendo sincera,
> e più e più entrava per lo raggio
> dell' lata luce, che da sè è vera.

And as I toward the goal of all desire
   Was drawing nigh, the ardor of my yearning
   In me died, as it must do,

. . . .

Because my vision, growing purified,
   Deeper and deeper entered in the beam
   Of the light profound, which is the Truth itself.

. . . .

> A quella luce cotal si diventa,
> che volgersi da lei per altro aspetto
> è impossibil che mai si consenta.

Però che il ben, ch' è del voler obbietto,
  tutto s'accoglie in lei, e fuor di quella
  è difettivo ciò che lì è perfetto.

From this light such doth a man become,
  That for another sight to turn from it
  His will could not consent.
Because the Good, which is the object of the will
  Is wholly gathered there, and that which there
  Is perfect, away from it imperfect is.

Ib. 46–48, 52–54, 100–105

But the vision of Beauty, Truth, Love, beheld in ecstatic contemplation, cannot be told; memory retains but little, and our speech cannot deliver what little may be remembered:

Omai sarà più corta mia favella,
  pure a quel ch'io ricordo, che di un fante
  che bagni ancor la lingua alla mammella.

And now my speech must fall more short
  Of what I still remember, than a babe's
  Whose tongue still nurses its mother's breast.

Ib. 106–108

And the great vision ends with a reiteration of the fundamental dogma of living faith, that the power which moves the universe is best interpreted by love,

l'amor che move il sole e l'altre stelle.

CHAPTER XIII

THE LAST YEARS

TOWARDS the end of his life Dante lived for a time at Verona, where Can Grande della Scala must have treated him with honorable distinction, for Dante reiterates his admiration and gratitude. And the last years he passed at Ravenna. Guido da Polenta, interesting to us as nephew of Francesca da Rimini, was lord of the city. In Dante's time, of all Italian cities, Ravenna, next to Rome, was richest in classical antiquities. The architectural monuments built during the brilliant period of the restoration of the Roman Empire in Italy by Justinian and during the reigns of his Gothic predecessors were far more ancient to Dante than Dante's times are to us. The Florence that Dante knew had nothing of the Florence we know but the Baptistery, the Bargello, and the Badia. Santa Maria del Fiore, Giotto's tower, the Palazzo Vecchio, Santa Croce, Santa Maria Novella (in its present form), Orsammichale, the churches and palaces of the Renaissance, have utterly changed the aspect of the city. But Ravenna had then the very basilicas, chapels, baptisteries, palaces, and campanili that tourists visit to-day, save only that time had buffeted them less. The Emperor Justinian and his Empress Theodora looked down upon Dante out of the mosaics in S. Vitale as somber and sad as they now look down on us; and not the least part of our interest in them is that he must have knelt, and said his prayers for the political regeneration of Italy, on the stone floor beneath them.

Here Dante lived in much honor but, it appears, in straitened circumstances, for tradition alleges that he taught poetry. His two sons and his daughter Beatrice joined him, but it would seem that they did not live together. And here he finished the *Divine Comedy*. These last years, to judge from the *Paradiso* and from some bantering bucolic poems which he exchanged with an ardent young classical scholar and poet, Giovanni del Virgilio, were calm and mellow. He knew that his work was done; he had experienced sin, suffering, purification, and the peace of complete acceptance of God's will, and he had embodied his experience in a poem that he felt to be sacred (*Par.* XXV, 1). He had cherished a hope that the renown of his poem would induce the Florentines to call him home and bestow the laurel crown upon him in the baptistery of San Giovanni (*Par.* XXV, 1–10 and Eclogue I); but that hope was vain, and he would not entertain the idea of being crowned in Bologna.

While at Ravenna, Dante made a visit to Verona, and there, before a distinguished audience, delivered a learned geological discourse to explain how it is that, although earth is heavier than water, so much of the earth's surface stands up above the level of the sea. He was also employed on at least one diplomatic errand for Count Guido Novello. The Doge of Venice, aggrieved by insults and injuries to her galleys and seamen by the people of Ravenna, declared war and stirred up the lords of the towns about Ravenna (for to be a neighbor meant to be unfriendly) to join him in hostilities against her. The situation was serious for Count Guido. He sent a hasty apology and promises of reparation; and selected Dante as envoy, on account of his talents and reputation, to help bring the quarrel to a peaceful conclusion. Dante went, and on his return journey caught a fever of which he died. Boccaccio tells of his death as follows:

"In the month of September, in the year of Christ 1321, on the day in which the Church celebrates the Exaltation of the Holy Cross, to the very great grief of Count Guido and, generally, of all the citizens of Ravenna, he gave up his weary spirit to the Creator; and I doubt not that it was received into the arms of the most noble Beatrice, with whom, in the sight of Him who is the Supreme God, having left the miseries of this present life, he now lives most joyfully in that life to whose felicity no end can be imagined. The magnanimous Knight [Count Guido] caused Dante's body on its bier to be dressed in the garb of a poet, and carried on the shoulders of the most distinguished citizens to the church of the Franciscan Friars in Ravenna, with the honors that he thought befitted such mortal remains; a procession followed it there, as if the state were mourning, and [the Count] had it laid in an ark of stone, in which it still lies. He then went back to the house in which Dante lived, and, according to the customs of Ravenna, delivered a long and elegant discourse, in praise of the profound learning and of the virtue of the deceased, as well as for the consolation of the friends whom he had left in bitter grief. And he made arrangements (if only his government and his life had lasted) to honor him with so remarkable a tomb, that had Dante possessed no other qualities to hand down his memory to future times, that would have done so." But Count Guido was driven out from Ravenna by his enemies, and his plan for a tomb got no further than a Latin epitaph written by Dante's friend, Giovanni del Virgilio. Later generations erected a tomb and monument; and there Dante's bones still lie.

The times and places when and where the *Comedy* was written are not known. Boccaccio reports this gossip: The first seven cantos of the *Inferno* had been written by Dante before his exile, and left behind in a chest; they were found by chance and sent after him, and the poet, urged by his friends, went on with the work. Boccaccio further reports that it was Dante's custom, when he had finished six or eight cantos, to send them on to Can Grande, who distributed copies of them. And he adds this curious story. "In this way [Dante] had sent to [Can Grande] all but the last thirteen cantos [of the *Paradiso*], which had been written but not sent on; and then it happened that he died, without leaving any memorandum of them. His children and pupils hunted through his papers, many times, for months, to see if he had not completed the work, but they could not find the remaining cantos in any way;

and they were in despair that they could not; and all his friends were greatly vexed that God had not left him in the world at least long enough to have finished the little that remained of his work. Dante's sons, Jacopo and Pietro, each of whom wrote verses, persuaded by some of their friends, made up their minds to supplement as well as they could, their father's work, so that it should not go forth in an imperfect state; when Jacopo, who was much more eager than the other, had a wonderful vision, which not only saved him from his foolish presumption, but also showed him where the thirteen cantos were, which the *Comedy* lacked and they had been unable to find.

"A worthy man of Ravenna, most respectable and trustworthy [and Boccaccio speaks of him elsewhere as one of the most intimate friends of Dante in Ravenna, and as having been with Dante in his last illness] — his name was Piero Giardino and he had been a pupil of Dante for a long time — used to tell this story. One night, eight months after his teacher's [i.e. Dante's] death, towards morning, Jacopo aforesaid came to his house, and said to him that, that night a little while before the time it was then, while he was asleep, he had seen his father Dante, dressed in very white garments and with a strange light shining in his countenance, come to him. He seemed to ask his father if he were alive and to hear from him the answer yes, but in the true life, not ours. Then, moreover, he seemed to ask his father also if he had finished his work before passing to the true life, and if he had finished it, where was the part that was lacking and that they had never been able to find. To this he seemed to hear an answer for the second time, 'Yes, I finished it.' And then it seemed to him that his father took him by the hand and led him into the room in which he used to sleep when he was living in this life; and touching one part of the room, said, 'What you have looked for so much is here.' After these words were said, it seemed to him that sleep and Dante departed at the same moment. Because of all this, he [i.e. Jacopo] asserted, that he could not keep from coming to see him to tell what he had seen, so that they should go together to look in the place shown him (which he had carefully noted in his memory) to see whether a true ghost or a false delusion had pointed it out. Wherefore, as there was still a good bit of night left, they went along together, and came to the house in which Dante was living when he died. They called the man who was then occupying the house, and were admitted. They went to the place indicated, and there they found a matting fastened to the wall, just as they had always seen it there in the past. This they lifted up gently, and saw a little recess in the wall which none of them had ever seen or known was there; and in it they found some manuscripts all moldy from the dampness of the wall, and close to being ruined if they had been left there any longer. They cleaned all the mold away, read the manuscripts and saw that they contained the thirteen cantos which they had looked for so much. So, perfectly delighted, they sent these, copied out, to Messer Can [Grande] according to the author's custom, and they were then added to the incomplete part where they belonged. In this way the work, put together in the course of years, was brought to completion" (*Trattatello in laude di Dante*, and the *Compendio*). As Boccaccio was personally acquainted with Piero Giardino, the story in its outline deserves to be believed.

Boccaccio, in his *Life of Dante*, also gives this familiar account of his appearance and ways: "Our poet was of medium height; and, after he had come to middle age, he was somewhat bent. In his movements he was serious and gentle, and he always wore very neat clothes, cut suitably according to his age. His face was long, his nose aquiline, his eyes rather big than little, large jaws, and his lower lip protruded beyond the upper. His coloring was dark, his hair and beard thick, black and curly, and there was always a thoughtful melancholy in his countenance. . . . In his manners at home and abroad he was wonderfully measured and self-contained, and most courteous and civil in every respect. He was very temperate in eating and drinking, going to his meals at the hours set, and not taking more than he needed. He was never an epicure either in eating or drinking; he praised the abstemious, generally ate simple food, and blamed exceedingly those who give a great part of their attention to procuring choice dishes and to seeing that they are cooked with great care, asserting that such people did not eat in order to live, but lived in order to eat. No one was more keen than he in his studies or whatever other interest occupied him; so much so that his wife and his household were often annoyed before they got used to his ways and had become indifferent to them. He seldom spoke unless he was spoken to, and then with consideration, adapting his voice to the subject of which he was talking; nevertheless, when it was appropriate, he was very eloquent and fluent in his discourse and had a ready and admirable delivery.

"In his youth he took the greatest pleasure in music and singing, and he used to frequent and make great friends with all the best singers and musicians. Prompted by the pleasure he got from this he composed many poems, which these friends, at his request, set to agreeable and admirable accompaniment. . . .

"He liked also to be by himself and away from people, so that his meditations should not be interrupted; and if any thought that interested him very much came to him while he was in company, no matter what might be said to him, he never answered a questioner, until his mind had approved or disapproved the thought. This often happened to him when he was at table, or travelling, or elsewhere.

"In his studies he was very assiduous, so that while he was busy over them, no news of any kind could stir him from them. As to this way of concentrating himself entirely on what interested him, this anecdote is told by reliable people. Once upon a time he was in Siena and happened upon an apothecary's shop, where he was given a book of great repute among men of parts, which (though promised to him sometime before) he had never seen.

It chanced that there was no other place for him
to go with the book, so he leaned against the counter
in front of the apothecary's, put the book before
him, and began to examine it most greedily. A little
while afterwards, in that same quarter of the town,
right in front of him, for it was a great holiday in
Siena, the young nobles held a kind of tournament,
and the people looking on made a tremendous noise
(shouting and playing all kinds of instruments as
their custom is), and all sorts of other things were
going on, such as dances by pretty ladies and games
by young men, that would draw anybody's attention; but nobody saw him stir or once lift up his
eyes from his book. On the contrary, although he had
taken his position there about noon, it was past
vespers, and he had looked through the whole book
and had got a summarized idea of it all, before he
got up; and when some people asked him how he
had been able to keep from looking at so beautiful
a show as had just passed before him, he answered
that he had noticed nothing."

The other biographers add little or nothing to
Boccaccio's description. As to the various portraits,
none were painted from Dante himself, but they all
appear to point to a common source, and therefore
deserve a fair measure of credit. The youthful portrait, attributed to Giotto, painted on the wall of the
chapel in the Bargello, now much altered from its
original condition, stands sorely, it seems to me, in
need of an elaborate defense. But even its apologists
will hardly claim that it was painted while Dante
was of that youthful age. For some two hundred

years there was a portrait on the wall of Santa
Croce, painted by Taddeo Gaddi, either from
description or from memory, but it was destroyed
in the sixteenth century. The death mask is not
genuine. For the lovers of Dante the bronze bust in
the museum at Naples is, however, an admirable
effigy to express Dante's character, and may well
remain his accepted likeness.

APPENDIX

SUGGESTIONS FOR BEGINNERS

THERE are many English translations of the *Divine Comedy*. With some of these, success seems to have been due to causes other than their intrinsic merits. Cary's was published early in the nineteenth century; it is in blank verse, faithful and forcible, and yet much of its popularity has come because it was virtually the first in the field. Longfellow's appeared shortly after our civil war; it is written in somewhat irregular blank verse, is conscientiously accurate, and was carried into favor by the prestige of his poetical reputation. Norton's was written about 1890; it is in a prose that follows the Italian text with scrupulous fidelity. These three are probably the translations best known in this country.

Translators are confronted at the outset by the question whether they shall follow Dante's form and write in *terza rima*, or boldly turn their backs on that difficulty and write in prose, or trim and adopt some riming or rhythmic measure intermediate between *terza rima* and prose. *Terza rima* is alien to the genius of the English language, whatever Lord Byron or Rupert Brooke may essay, or Shelley in a fragment may achieve. English syllables end in consonants; whereas in Italian four words out of five end in vowels, and those that end in a consonant trail softly away in an *r* or an *l*. This difference renders the use of those intricately interwoven rimes of *terza rima* quite out of the question in English, although they have been often tried, for instance by Cayley, Plumptre, and Haselfoot; and the same may be said of the fantastic translation in rime by C. L. Shadwell.

On the other hand, to translate poetry composed with rhythm and rime into prose is to confess an astonishing degree of inadequacy, an inadequacy that may be measured by supposing the contrary process, for instance, that a Frenchman were to translate Bacon's *Essays* into alexandrine verse.

173

There remains then the *via media*, and that in English must be blank verse. This measure is freighted with all the authority of the greatest tradition in English literature; in it Shakespeare, Milton, Wordsworth wrote, and from the days of our earliest acquaintance with poetry we are taught to regard it as the appropriate verse for heroic themes. Blank verse is — it should seem beyond question — the proper medium for a translation of Dante. And if any readers propose to confine themselves to English, they should take a version done in blank verse.

But nobody who wishes to know Dante will confine himself to an English version. Poetry is the wedded union of words and music. Music lies in the order of words; and beauty, strength, and vividness of language lie both in the choice of words and in their order when chosen. Masters of language instinctively feel the relations between each word and those which precede and follow it. As Coleridge says, poetry is the best words in the best order. The best order of words in English is a very bad order in Italian, and the best order of words in Italian is feeble and unintelligible in English. There seems little room here for difference of opinion. Dante says: "Let everyone know that nothing which hath the harmony of musical connection can be transferred from its own tongue into another without shattering all its sweetness and harmony" (*Conv.* I, 7). The reader may accept for certain that in every English version the harmony and sweetness of Dante's poetry lie shattered, even when, as in Rossetti's translations of sonnets and canzoni, there is an English harmony and an English sweetness.

It is true that many people, who have not the leisure to study Italian, would like to know something of the *Divine Comedy;* it seems also to be true that almost everybody who has the leisure and inclination to study Italian likes to begin with the *Divine Comedy.* In either case, let the neophyte get Professor Henry Johnson's or Professor Courtney Langdon's translation, or, as more portable — making in every way less demand on the pocket — the edition of the *Divine Comedy* published in the Temple Classics; then let him read the English story, and every now and again, when he is stirred by a special passage, line or word, let him turn to the Italian, which he will find printed on the opposite page. He would do equally well, indeed in some respects better, to take W. W. Vernon's *Readings* on the *Inferno*, the *Purgatorio*, and the *Paradiso;* or A. J. Butler's edition. These books have the translation on the same page, and long comments and elucidations as well.

The beginner may know nothing of Italian, but the mere uttering aloud, even if with horrible mispronunciation, of Italian syllables that were written by Dante, in the very language spoken by him, by Beatrice, by Brunetto Latini, by Farinata, by Ugolino, by Francesca da Rimini, conjures up over the page a lovely haze such as lingers over the Arno, when the evening star looks down, of a June evening, after the sun has set.

For the English-speaking foreigner Italian words have all the charm of Italy. They are fragrant with her fragrance, beautiful with her beauty; they call up before our imaginations all we have seen or heard or read of Italy — the Bay of Naples, the stark Apennines, the stone pines, the romantic architecture, the frescoed walls, the world-famous rivers, the plains of Umbria, the trellised vineyards. They walk across the printed page like gay masqueraders, or when serious, with a solemnity that our English words have lost through familiarity. English words, read in the papers and heard daily bandied about, lose their bloom, they become hackneyed, stale; but to the sensitive beginner the novel Italian words are of an exquisite rarity and pregnant with meaning. And a chance recognition of a new word through its Latin origin or its French relationship, makes it warmly welcome. I suspect that the English student, in the sentimental first stage of his acquaintance with Dante, gets far more significance from the Italian words than Italian youths do. At any rate, a translation in itself is a dead thing; it cannot be the equivalent of living Italian. Indeed, it is impossible to say how barren is the English version without the Italian text to look at, and how amazing a richness is conferred by merely an occasional glance at the Italian.

This little book has been prepared for readers, bred upon

the religious and scientific ideas of modern times, who seek
a spiritual meaning in Dante and are indifferent to thirteenth-
century theology and astronomy; and so it counsels such
readers to skim lightly over Dante's elaborate reckonings of
the time of day, his explanations of the density of the moon
or the influences of the stars, and all natural history taken
from Aristotle. From this point of view, for proper reading
introductory to Dante, the beginner should go to Isaiah, the
Psalms, St. Paul, Plotinus, St. Augustine's *Confessions*, or
rather, to selected parts of such books, also to the Lives of
St. Catherine of Siena, of St. Theresa, and to passages from
Ruysbroeck, from the Lady Juliana of Norwich, Brother
Lawrence, and St. John of the Cross, as well as to sundry
chapters of Miss Underhill's book *Mysticism*.

Dante is a prophet of the spiritual life, and he is best understood, not by studying Benvenuto da Imola, Witte, Scartazzini, Moore, Gardner, and other eminent scholars and
commentators, but by making ourselves familiar with the
thoughts of those men who held the same spiritual view of
life that Dante did.

Nobody who has any knowledge of Dante or any acquaintance with the bulky literature of explanation that encircles
him, can entertain any feeling other than deep respect and
gratitude to the scholars who have dedicated their lives to the
service of the great poet. They constitute the goodly company
of *amici della Memoria di Dante*, for we may well apply to
them the title assumed by Leonardo Bruni. They have cleared
away difficulties in the text; they have elucidated the meaning
of old words; they have tracked to their sources a thousand
references and allusions taken by Dante from all the known
literature that existed before him; they have, as it were,
digged, drained, and reclaimed a great part of the slough of
obscurity that surrounded the sacred poem, so that now we
all, if we will, may approach it over a solid road of scholarship.
Not to mention their labors, even in a little elementary book
like this, would be to slam the door in the face of intellectual
curiosity. But the palace of learning is like a mediaeval castle,
with outer courts, inner courts, halls, chambers, corridors,
intricate passage-ways, and underground vaults, where duly

authorized ciceroni only are competent to guide and explain; a primer can but point the finger in certain directions and offer certain general suggestions.

The beginner should read certain essays on Dante that have become classical; that by Thomas Carlyle on *The Hero as a Poet* and those by R. W. Church, James Russell Lowell, and Charles Eliot Norton. C. A. Dinsmore's *Aids to the Study of Dante* is an unusually good book. The beginner should buy the three little volumes of the Temple Classics which contain the *Inferno*, the *Purgatorio*, and the *Paradiso*, Italian on one side, English on the other, and also the volume that contains the *Vita Nuova* and the *Canzoniere;* and whenever he goes for a solitary walk, of a Sunday or in his holidays, he should carry one of them in his pocket.

Beyond this no primer should be dogmatic, but a bit of advice may be given. Let the beginner go to some library, such for instance as the Harvard College library, take down from the shelves a volume or two of the early commentators, and dip into them, however casually; for there is in their ancient pages an odor of reverence, of filial piety, that communicates itself through the touch of the hands and the look of the paragraphs, and the visitor — as if he were in some religious building in a foreign land — cannot but feel a soothing calm from the consciousness that he is in the midst of disciples of a very great man. Here is a list of those earliest commentators:

Chiose Anonime alla prima Cantica della Divina Commedia (Ed. Selmi, 1865). This gloss is believed to be the earliest, and has been assigned, at a guess, to the year 1320.

Il Commento all' Inferno di Graziuolo de' Bambaglioli (Udine, 1892). This is assigned to the year 1324 or thereabouts.

Chiose alla Cantica dell' Inferno di Dante Allighieri attribuite a Jacopo suo figlio (Florence, 1848). This is of about the same date.

Commento di Jacopo di Giovanni dalla Lana (Milan, 1865). Probably written a little before 1330.

L' Ottimo Commento della Divina Commedia (Pisa, 1827). Written, perhaps by Andrea Lancia, a little after 1330.

Petri Allegherii Commentarium (Florence, 1845). This is a

commentary on the whole *Comedy* by Dante's son Pietro; it was composed about 1340.

Il Comento sopra la Commedia di Dante Alighieri di Giovanni Boccaccio. (There are various editions.) This contains the substance of Boccaccio's lectures in 1373; it ends abruptly, owing to his death, in Canto XVII of the *Inferno*.

Benvenuti de Rambaldis de Imola Comentum super Dantis Aldigherij Comœdiam (Florence, 1887). This was written in 1375.

Divers sorts of curiosity take the beginner to one or another of these commentaries; one is the oldest, one by Dante's son, another (that by Benvenuto da Imola) is by far the longest and the best, a fourth was written by that attractive person, Giovanni Boccaccio; two are in Latin, the rest in Italian. The beginner will do no more than read a few lines here and there; and, even at that, he should be on his guard, and remember to make allowance for the changed significance of words. These old commentators all call Beatrice Theology, whereas we should call her the Knowledge of God or better still, the Wisdom of Love, for God is Love; to them Theology was a radiant light, but to us it usually recalls Faust's remark, when enumerating his studies, — Philosophy, Jurisprudence, Medicine, *"und leider auch Theologie."*

Sometimes the beginner has a curiosity to know at least the names of Dante's early biographers. They are:

Giovanni Villani (1275?–1348); *Cronica*, Book VIII, Chap. 49. A very brief account of the poet and his works.

Giovanni Boccaccio (1313–1375); *Trattatello in laude di Dante*, a *Little Treatise in praise of Dante*, written about 1364; and the *Compendio*, which is the *Trattatello* with variations of no great importance, apparently made not by Boccaccio but by some unknown hand.

Filippo Villani, a nephew of Giovanni (d. about 1310); *De Vita et Moribus Dantis*, a brief biography included with others of illustrious Florentines.

Leonardo Bruni, also called Lionardo Aretino (1370–1444); *La Vita di Dante*. Bruni had before him some original documents unknown to Boccaccio.

These, together with several fifteenth-century biographies, and some scattered scraps concerning Dante's life, are published together in a large volume, in the *Storia Letteraria d'Italia*. Of them all Boccaccio's is by far the best, and Bruni's next; these two have been translated by J. Robinson Smith (H. Holt, 1901), and by P. H. Wicksteed (Chatto and Windus, 1911). The other biographies have little value.

For the reader who merely desires a brief account of what is known of Dante and his times, there are several little books: *Dante Alighieri, his Life and Works*, by Paget Toynbee; *Dante*, by E. G. Gardner; *Dante*, by C. H. Grandgent. There are also, of course, very large books with full exposition of the evidence concerning the events of Dante's life, such as *Dante; sein Leben und sein Werk*, etc., by Franz Xaver Kraus (1897), or *Dante*, by Nicola Zingarelli in the *Storia Letteraria d'Italia*.

But I have more than reached my limit, and I bid the student Godspeed upon his more ambitious road,

> *lo tuo piacere omai prendi per duce.*

He will sit at the feet of Karl Witte (the great German scholar, with his *Dante-Forschungen*), of Scartazzini, the Swiss, who wrote in German and Italian, of Karl Vossler, an authority now living, of Dante's countrymen, Pio Rajna, Corrado Ricci, Tommaso Casini, Francesco Torraca, of the learned Englishmen, E. Moore, Paget Toynbee, E. G. Gardner, P. H. Wicksteed, and of other scholars, whose reputations are now in the making, both English and American. He will take from the shelf the three concordances, *Concordance of the Divina Commedia*, by E. A. Fay, *Concordanza delle opere Italiane in prosa e del canzoniere di Dante Alighieri*, by E. S. Sheldon and A. C. White, and *Dantis Alagherii Operum Latinorum Concordantiae*, by E. K. Rand, E. H. Wilkins, and A. C. White. But I have already gone too far, and I obey the Scholar's voice that sternly addresses me and my fellow dilettanti:

> *O voi, che siete in piccioletta barca,*
> *tornate a riveder li vostri liti.*

INDEX

ALLEGORY, in the Middle Ages, 39.
Apocalypse, 18–19.
Augustine, St., his conversion, 21–22; on sin, 80; on lust, 85; on prayer, 101; conversation with Monica on "Enter thou into the joy of thy Lord," 138–140.

BEATRICE (see also Vita Nuova), 23; in *Purgatorio* her rebuke to Dante, 43–46.
Benvenuto da Imola, 5.
Bernard, St., 159; his prayer to the Virgin Mary, 159–160.
Boccaccio, biography of Dante, 4; lectures on Dante, 5; on Dante's studious youth, 36; on allegory, 39; on Dante's licentiousness, 42; on his pride, 86–87; on Dante's death and funeral, 165–166; description of Dante, 169–170; anecdote of his powers of concentration, 170–171.
Bochme, Jacob, on self-surrender, 132.
Boethius, quoted, 136.
Bonagiunta, 119–120.
Bonaventura, St., on drawing near to God, 137.
Boniface VIII, Pope, 18.
Botticelli, 5.
Brunetto Latini, relations to Dante, 23–24.
Bruni, Leonardo, 5; on Dante's youth, 34; on his priorate, 48; on Dante's drawing, 79.
Butler, A. J., 175.
Bunyan, his conversion, 22; on sin, 81.
Byron, on Dante's tenderness, 11.

CACCIAGUIDA, 151.
Can Grande, Dante's letter to, 40.
Carlyle, John A., 9.
Carlyle, Thomas, 9.
Carpenter, Boyd, Bishop of Ripon, 1.